MODERN POTLUCK

MODERN POTLUCK

BEAUTIFUL FOOD TO SHARE

KRISTIN DONNELLY

CLARKSON POTTER/PUBLISHERS
NEW YORK

All rights reserved.
Published in the United States by Clarkson Potter/
Publishers, an imprint of the Crown Publishing Group, a
division of Penguin Random House LLC, New York.
www.crownpublishing.com
www.clarksonpotter.com

CLARKSON POTTER is a trademark and POTTER with
colophon is a registered trademark of Penguin Random
House LLC.

Library of Congress Cataloging-in-Publication Data
Donnelly, Kristin, author.
Modern potluck / Kristin Donnelly.—
First edition.
   Includes index.
 1. Make-ahead cooking. 2. Entertaining. I. Title.
 TX714.D5454 2016
 641.5'55—dc23   2015026808

ISBN 978-0-8041-8711-4
eBook ISBN 978-0-8041-8712-1

Printed in China

Book design by Jan Derevjanik
Cover design by Jan Derevjanik
Cover photograph by Yossy Arefi

10 9 8 7 6 5 4 3 2 1

First Edition

To Elsa, for inspiring this book,
and to Phil, for convincing me to write it

CONTENTS

INTRODUCTION

I grew up in the suburbs of Philadelphia with nine aunts and uncles and fifteen cousins all within a half-hour's drive, so every family gathering—from Thanksgiving to an eight-year-old's birthday party—was, basically, a potluck. Each little tribe usually would make the same few dishes for about a decade (spinach dip in a bread bowl and chicken liver mousse with wine-soaked figs are a couple of perennial favorites) before finally tiring of it and trying something new.

When I was in high school, I sang in a twenty-member a cappella group, and once a year, I'd get a glimpse of a more traditional community potluck. We used to sing at a Quaker meetinghouse, and at the end, the members would invite us to eat with them. A series of folding tables lined with gingham cloths groaned under the weight of many covered platters of salads and oven-to-table casseroles. I loved lifting the lids on each of those dishes to see what was beneath. It was often something creamy and starchy— rich, cheesy gratins; sweet creamed corn; classic green bean casserole topped with French's fried onions. It was a party that definitely relied on more than a few cans of condensed soup.

Thanks to my upbringing, I never knew much about throwing a formal dinner party—the kind with menus and place settings—until I became an editor in my mid-twenties at *Food & Wine* magazine. There, we would produce stories about *perfect* hosts who could give us *amazing* ideas that we had *never seen before.* At first, I felt inspired by those stories, and no matter how small my apartment was in New York, I would always try to replicate this style of entertaining. I'd obsess over the guest list (should it be people who know one another or who don't?) and the food (I'd often focus on what was available *that day* at the farmers' market, driving myself insane when the ramps I needed for the gnocchi were scooped up by all the chefs).

After I had my daughter, Elsa, those types of dinner parties seemed not just daunting but also impossible. Because I couldn't eat at restaurants as much as I used to, I felt that my social life was starting to fall apart. That's when I remembered potlucks. What a brilliant idea! I could focus my energy on making one dish and get a full meal in return, all the while hanging out with my friends or meeting my neighbors.

I used to feel a bit embarrassed about

anymore. In an era of artisan pickles, gluten-free diets, #foodporn hashtags, pastured eggs, and kimchi tacos, the potluck has become potentially quite complicated. Now you have to consider things like dietary restrictions and Instagram worthiness. There's also pressure to make a standout dish to serve people who are way savvier about food than they were a few decades ago. Plus, you might be judged not only by how tasty your dish is but also by how sustainable. ("So, did you buy your pork shoulder right from the farmer? It's Berkshire, right?")

I wrote *Modern Potluck* to give people updated, foolproof, crowd-pleasing recipes that will hold up on the buffet table and are also just a little bit impressive. I want to inspire those cooks who tend to always bring the same thing, as well as cooks who are always looking for something new. And to make the book itself a kind of potluck, I asked some of my very favorite home cooks to contribute their best party recipes. You'll find them scattered throughout, and their collective advice and dishes are invaluable.

Like most people who write cookbooks, my greatest wish is to bring people together around food in a way that's as easy and fun as possible. The secret to doing this is to share the work with your guests. And, as it turns out, guests love it that way, too.

not having grown up knowing how to throw a proper dinner party. But then I realized that, at the magazine, we write stories about parties for 8 or 12 guests. My mom could throw a party for 50 or even 100 without having a panic attack. Her secret (in addition to some serious planning) was the potluck, of course.

Pondering further, I began to realize that maybe potlucks weren't so simple

A COOK'S NOTES

ON WHAT "MODERN" MEANS

During the past decade or so, there has been a shift in the way many Americans eat. People are adding far more vegetables and other plant-based foods to their plates. They're seeking out meat, dairy, and eggs from animals raised sustainably. They're also more open to ingredients from around the world, like the North African spice paste called harissa and the funky Southeast Asian fish sauce. The "modern" in this book's title addresses all these factors—including that we're more adventurous than ever about our food, but in some ways also more restrictive.

I'm an unabashed omnivore. I don't shun any particular ingredients, although the recipes in this book generally avoid processed foods. I emphasize vegetables, legumes, and whole grains, but you'll still find quite a bit of meat, seafood, and dairy. To make these recipes healthier than their classic counterparts, I use fewer fatty ingredients like cream or bacon, but for the sake of taste, I also don't use faux healthy ingredients like low-fat cheese. If you're going to indulge, just do it and enjoy it; then have a kale salad tomorrow.

The recipes in this book don't conform to a specific diet, but I've noted when they are or can be adapted to be gluten-free, vegetarian, or vegan.

Because I know many potluck meals involve children, I've generally kept the spice level of the recipes low, allowing the cook to add more heat to fit the crowd.

ON SERVING SIZE

For this book particularly, serving size can sometimes be complicated. Are you making the dish as one of a few offerings, or will it be one of twenty platters on the table? At large potlucks, with a huge variety of dishes, people tend to take a small spoonful or slice of everything, and then maybe go back for seconds of something that was exceptionally delicious. Because of this ambiguity, I've noted a fairly large range of serving sizes, and when appropriate, I have noted the approximate total volume of the recipe.

ON SEASONING AND DEVELOPING FLAVOR

Good seasoning—the process of adding salt, spices, acid, and herbs to make food taste better—is what can often separate a fine cook from a good one and a good cook from a great one.

In my experience, many home cooks don't use enough salt. Sometimes, health is cited as the concern, and this can be a valid reason for taking it easy on the salt. But the goal is never to make food that tastes salty; instead, you want to make food that tastes like a better version of itself. The best-tasting food is often salted multiple times during the preparation—as you sweat the onions, before you brown the meat, before you serve the dish.

When I tell people they need to use more salt, they often ask me, "Well, how much?" That's tricky, too. People have different palates, and different salts have different levels of salinity, so it's best for cooks to learn to season food their own way. For that reason, unless the recipe involves seasoning a raw meat mixture that you can't fix later, or something else that would be dangerous to taste while raw, I avoid specifying the exact amount of salt to use. Rather, I guide you about when to season.

If you're seasoning the dish in its final stage, add a little salt at a time, until it tastes good. If you're seasoning meat before you brown it, or vegetables before you roast them, use enough salt so you see a light dusting, then proceed.

This brings me to types of salt. Ordinary table salt has a harsh, unpleasant iodine flavor, so I don't recommend cooking with it. Some people prefer to use sea salt because it has beneficial minerals and more interesting, subtle flavors. Note, though, that the salinity of these salts can vary widely, so if you want to use sea salt, taste your food frequently to get a sense of how it's developing its flavor. For general seasoning, I recommend kosher salt because it's visible on the surface of the food and easy to add in pinches. For sprinkling on at the end, I like to use a flaky salt, like Maldon.

One more thing to note: not all kosher salts are the same. I tested these recipes with Morton's kosher salt, which is heavier by volume than Diamond Crystal salt. This means if you add ¼ teaspoon Morton's to a recipe and ¼ teaspoon of Diamond Crystal to the same recipe, the one with Morton's will taste saltier.

In the end, when it comes to the type of salt you want to use, pick one and stick with it. That way, you'll have a consistent sense for how much you need to add.

Seasoning, of course, is not just about salt. Acid, from citrus and vinegars, adds pop to a dish. And heat, from chiles or peppercorns, doesn't have to obliterate the flavor of food or your taste buds; used carefully, it can enliven a dish. Herbs,

spices, garlic, and onions, as well as condiments (which add lots of different flavors at once), help season food as well.

Apart from seasoning, browning your ingredients brings out those foods' natural sugars and is an important part of developing the flavor for certain recipes. I talk more about this when presenting the stew recipes (see page 97).

Ultimately, the goal here is for you to trust these recipes but also use your intuition. If a dish seems like it could use more flavor, try adding some salt, a squeeze of lemon, or a squirt of Sriracha. If you wish the dish had more depth, maybe add a dash of soy sauce or brown the meat or vegetables more next time. The more you play with seasoning, the more you'll learn and the better your food will taste.

ON GARNISHING

Garnishes, including fresh herbs, toasted nuts or seeds, crumbled bacon, and chopped or sliced crunchy vegetables, add extra pops of flavor and texture to the food. They also make dishes more visually appealing. For example, a homey (and homely) dish like the Tomatillo Pulled Chicken (page 96) becomes photo-worthy when topped with a few sliced radishes, some sour cream, and a sprinkling of cilantro leaves. Taking the time to garnish food just before serving or offering some garnishes at the table will make a dish that much more tasty.

RULES OF THE POTLUCK

I'm still a magazine editor at heart, so I love lists. Here are a few that will help with planning your next potluck.

WHAT MAKES FOR A GREAT POTLUCK DISH?

1. **IT WILL HOLD UP ON A BUFFET TABLE.** Anything that needs to be served hot but can't be kept hot without overcooking—steaks (unless you want them at room temperature, of course) and many fish dishes, for example—is best saved for your intimate dinner party. Similarly, stick with sturdier salads rather than those made with lots of delicate greens, which wilt quickly.

2. **IT HAS THREE COMPONENTS, MAX.** Potlucks are the time for fun, unfussy dishes. It's fine to bring along an extra dressing, sauce, or garnish to be added at the table, but try to keep the extras to one or two.

3. **IT'S CROWD PLEASING WITH JUST A HINT OF EDGE.** My mom used to tell me to bring fairly bland dishes to parties because not everyone likes spicy or overtly seasoned food. Thankfully, people now enjoy lots of different flavors. Nevertheless, a potluck with people you don't know well might *not* be the time to bring that tripe recipe you've always wanted to try.

WHAT HOSTS AND ORGANIZERS SHOULD KNOW

1. **CONTROL YOUR INNER CONTROL FREAK.** Dinner parties are the time you can mastermind every dish and style the look of your table. But when you're hosting a potluck, relax. Sure, you can *suggest* that someone bring a certain type of dish, but if your friend is dying to bring her famous (infamous?) macaroni salad, just let her bring it (or gently suggest the Fregola with Tuna, Capers, and Slow-Roasted Tomatoes on page 64).

   To make sure the party doesn't have six platters of deviled eggs (unless you're having a deviled egg potluck, which is a brilliant idea, thanks!), you might want to create a sign-up sheet (setting up a spreadsheet on Google Drive that everyone can access works well). Again, there's no need to be overly controlling—just create a list of categories, such as Dips & Hors d'Oeuvres; Salads and Vegetables; Main Dishes; Desserts; Other, and let your guests fill in from there.

2. **KEEP YOUR GUESTS IN THE LOOP ABOUT DIETARY RESTRICTIONS.** If you know that some people at the party can't eat certain foods, it's nice to tell the other guests so they can consider this as they choose their dishes. Make it clear that their dishes do not need to be gluten-free or vegan (unless it *is* an absolute must).

3. **PICK A THEME, OR DON'T.** If you host potlucks regularly, choosing a theme can be a fun way of mixing it up. But it's also unnecessary and perhaps even unadvisable for those larger potlucks with lots of unknown guests. If you do want to go the theme route, here are some ideas.

   - Global street food: You can ask people to bring a dish that is inspired by one they discovered on their travels or from a place they want to go.

- Your grandmother's favorite recipe, your way: Ask people to bring the original recipe to display alongside their updates.

- Book club: Bring people together around a certain cookbook, or if you're reading fiction, ask guests to make recipes inspired by the book.

- Seasonal parties: In the summer, ask people to make dishes that use things from the garden or lots of herbs. In winter, throw a soup party and assign half to bring soups and the other half to bring accompaniments, like bread and desserts.

- Wine-pairing potluck: Tell everyone to make a dish and bring a wine that pairs well with it.

- Swap parties: In addition to a dish, ask guests to bring gently used clothes, kitchen items, books, or even excess garden produce to swap.

- Stand the heat: If your group is a lot of spicy food lovers, have them make dishes that use different kinds of chiles. Then, serve ice cream and sorbet for dessert.

- Local pride: Ask your guests to create dishes using one of their favorite local ingredients or food products.

4. **THINK ABOUT THE FLOW AND LABEL THE FOOD:** For a small potluck, putting most of the food on the same table is fine and makes sense. But for a larger one, it's usually easier to divide the food among different tables and different spaces. For example, you could put all the vegetarian food in one place or divide the dishes on tables designated for hot and cold food, or starters and main dishes. If there will be several hot dishes, put down trivets so they have easy spots to land. Have blank tags and pens ready so you or your guests can write down the name of the dish and include any necessary information, like "contains nuts!" or "spicy!" or "gluten-free!" For even more fun, line your tables with butcher paper and encourage people to describe their dishes right alongside, on the paper.

5. **DON'T FORGET PLATES, CUPS, NAPKINS, AND UTEN-SILS:** Unless you ask people to bring these things, it's your job to make sure they're on hand. For larger parties, disposable plates and utensils are easiest, and if you're willing to splurge a bit, bamboo or palm leaf plates and wooden utensils are a great choice; they're durable, pretty, and compostable. To help with the flow of traffic, set up a spot for plates and napkins and use trays or jars for holding utensils. High-quality disposable cups are a bit harder to come by. If you have the space and you entertain often, it might be worth investing in a set of washable plastic wineglasses and other types of cups. You can ask people to bring serving utensils—large spoons, pie servers, knives—appropriate for their dishes, but have extras on hand in case they forget. Remember to also have visible receptacles for garbage, and if you want to allow for recycling or composting, label the containers clearly.

6. **MAKE SURE YOUR KITCHEN IS AS CLEAN AS YOU CAN MANAGE:** People will inevitably want to reheat their dishes or garnish them at the last minute, so try to have clear counters.

7. **STOCK THE BAR:** Even if you don't have a formal bar, create an area for drinks that includes a large ice chest, cups, and wine and beer openers. Think about how you want to handle water, as well—you can either buy bottled water in bulk or, more sustainable, set out large, refillable containers of water with spigots.

8. **IF YOU'RE HOSTING OR ORGANIZING A POTLUCK OFFSITE, FIND OUT WHAT'S AVAILABLE:** Ask about running water, electricity, bathrooms, garbage cans, tables, and seating in advance, so you're not surprised the day of your event. You will likely need to bring coolers for drinks and perishable food, as well as garbage bags.

WHAT GUESTS SHOULD KNOW

1. **ASK IN ADVANCE ABOUT USING THE OVEN (OR THE GRILL OR THE STOVE):** If your dish has any last-minute prep, or you want to serve in a slow cooker that requires an outlet, ask your host in advance to make sure there is space. Otherwise, switch gears and choose a different dish.

2. **THINK ABOUT HOW YOU'LL TRANSPORT YOUR FOOD:** If the dish is not easy to carry itself, place it in a box. For an investment of about $20, you can buy an insulated casserole carrier. Alternatively, you can wrap your hot or cold dish in newspaper, a natural insulator, and then a few blankets.

3. **ASK ABOUT DIETARY RESTRICTIONS:** This isn't an absolute must, but in this era of so many food intolerances, it's considerate of other guests to check if gluten or dairy or nuts or meat might be a problem for some people.

4. **IF YOU SIGN UP TO BRING SOMETHING, BRING IT, ESPECIALLY IF IT'S CRUCIAL TO THE PARTY:** A party without the napkins you said you'd bring is no fun at all.

5. **BRING SERVING UTENSILS:** To make the host's life easier, bring a knife for your cake or pie, tongs or spoons for your salad, and so on. Extra credit goes to guests who bring their dishes in the vessels that are also used for serving.

6. **TAKE YOUR PLATTER HOME:** Unless the host offers, don't leave your platter or bowls behind for the host to clean. Instead, take it with you, washing it only if you can sneak in a minute to do so at the host's house.

SOME NOTES ABOUT FOOD SAFETY

Food safety is no joking matter. It's important when you're making food anytime, but it's especially critical when you're feeding a crowd.

One of the main causes of food poisoning is cross contamination. Any tool or surface that comes into contact with raw meat, fish, shellfish, poultry, or eggs, including your hands, should be cleaned with hot soapy water immediately afterward. Also, the tongs used to turn half-cooked meat or shellfish should not also be used for serving a salad (or to handle the cooked protein) without being thoroughly cleaned first.

Food temperature is also important. Prepared food can usually stay safely at room temperature for up to two hours, but if it's over 90 degrees where you are serving, then figure that it's really only safe for one hour. (Foods that have a high-acid dressing or sauce or sugary foods, like desserts, are often exceptions to this rule.) Until you are ready to serve, keep hot food hot (at a temperature higher than 140°F) and cold food cold (40°F or cooler). Alternatively, you can serve hot food from a slow cooker or a chafing dish; similarly, you can set a bowl for a chilled salad over a shallow baking dish full of ice.

Sometimes, the biggest culprits in incidents of food poisoning are the ones you'd least suspect. For example, low-acid starchy foods, like potatoes, beans, and rice, can breed bacteria at room temperature. (Believe it or not, food poisoning from potato salad is more often caused by the potatoes than by the mayo.) Be vigilant about how long the food stays out, and wash all tools, including your hands, often as you prep the food.

SNACKS, DIPS & DRINKS

SWEET-SPICY-SALTY SNACK MIX

VEGETARIAN; GLUTEN-FREE (OPTIONAL) / MAKES 3 HEAPING QUARTS

12 CUPS UNSALTED OR LIGHTLY SALTED POPCORN (SEE NOTE)

2 OUNCES RICE CRACKERS, BROKEN INTO BITE-SIZE PIECES (ABOUT 2 CUPS)

½ CUP (1 STICK) UNSALTED BUTTER

1 CUP LIGHT BROWN SUGAR

¼ CUP LIGHT CORN SYRUP

2 TABLESPOONS SOY SAUCE

½ TEASPOON BAKING SODA

¼ TEASPOON CAYENNE PEPPER

⅛ TEASPOON CREAM OF TARTAR

¾ CUP PUMPKIN SEEDS

½ CUP SUNFLOWER SEEDS

2 TABLESPOONS SESAME SEEDS

Popcorn, rice crackers, and a mixture of seeds get mixed with a soy-caramel sauce for a gluten-free (if you use gluten-free soy sauce) and nut-free snack mix that's hard to stop eating. While the mix is sweet enough to serve as dessert, the cayenne heat makes it great with cocktails.

NOTE. Twelve cups of popcorn is the approximate amount in 1 standard microwave bag. To make popcorn on the stovetop, combine ¼ cup grapeseed oil, coconut oil, or other high-heat oil with 3 kernels in a large, heavy pot over high heat. When those kernels pop, add the remaining kernels in a single layer and remove the pot from the heat. Count to 30, and then return the pot to the heat. The popcorn should start popping rapidly; when the popping slows to a near stop, turn off the heat. Uncover the pot when the popcorn has fully stopped popping. Carefully transfer the hot popcorn to a bowl.

Preheat the oven to 225°F. Line a large rimmed baking sheet with parchment paper or a Silpat pan liner.

In a very large bowl, toss the popcorn with the rice crackers.

In a medium saucepan, melt the butter. Add the brown sugar and corn syrup and cook over medium-high heat, stirring constantly, until the sugar is melted and a deep amber syrup forms, about 4 minutes. Stir in the soy sauce, baking soda, cayenne, and cream of tartar. Slowly and carefully pour the syrup over the popcorn and crackers, and stir to coat. When nearly evenly coated, stir in the seeds.

Spread the mixture on the prepared baking sheet. Bake for about 1 hour, until dry to the touch. Let cool to room temperature. Break the snack mix into bite-size pieces and serve.

POTLUCK PREP. The snack mix can be kept in an airtight container for 3 to 5 days. If it gets sticky (this can happen if it's humid), dry it again briefly in a 225°F oven.

PIG CANDY

GLUTEN-FREE / MAKES 16 PIECES

½ CUP LIGHT BROWN SUGAR

¼ TEASPOON CAYENNE
PEPPER

16 (1-OUNCE) STRIPS OF
BACON (1 POUND)

1 TABLESPOON SHERRY
VINEGAR

Candied bacon is a fantastic snack to eat with drinks because it hits so many spots on the tongue: It's sweet, smoky, and salty, and usually a little spicy. I add another element to make it even harder to stop eating: tangy sherry vinegar. The hardest part of this recipe is waiting for the bacon to fully cool and crisp before trying it. For the most evenly cooked bacon, use bacon that's the same width on either end.

Preheat the oven to 375°F.

In a small bowl, toss the brown sugar with the cayenne.

Line 2 baking sheets with foil and arrange the bacon on them in a single layer. Lightly brush the tops of the bacon with the vinegar and sprinkle with all of the sugar mixture, rubbing it into an even layer on each strip.

Bake for 10 minutes. Change the position of the baking sheets on the oven racks and turn them from back to front. Bake for another 5 minutes and start checking the bacon. You want to pull it out when the strips are dark brown and nearly crisp but not blackened (a few black spots are okay). It should take between 16 and 20 minutes total. Watch carefully, as the bacon can go from perfect to blackened in a minute.

Arrange a cooling rack (or 2, if you have them) over a sheet of foil.

Using tongs, transfer the bacon to the rack, dab off any fat from the bacon with paper towels, and let cool completely.

POTLUCK PREP. The pig candy is best the day it's made but will hold up for several hours at room temperature. After it's cool and crisp, you can bring it to the party loosely wrapped in foil and serve standing up in cocktail cups.

DEVILED EGGS FOR EVERY SEASON

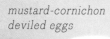

mustard-cornichon deviled eggs

green deviled eggs and ham

bloody mary deviled eggs

smoky deviled eggs with toasted rosemary

Deviled eggs aren't just retro, they're ancient. There's evidence that the ancient Romans ate boiled eggs with spicy sauces at the beginning of their meals. When I was growing up, deviled eggs were almost always the same: a little too much mayonnaise with just a whisper of paprika and not enough salt. I could take them or leave them. Then I tried chef April Bloomfield's version at her New York City restaurant, The Spotted Pig, where the eggs are luscious and punchy at the same time, and I became a convert.

While the four recipes here were inspired by the seasons, each is great served any time of year.

TIPS FOR AMAZING DEVILED EGGS

1. Follow the instructions below for making perfect hard-boiled eggs.

2. If you like the filling fluffy and evenly mashed, press the egg yolks through a sieve before mixing in the remaining ingredients, or puree all of the ingredients in a food processor.

3. Use more acid and salt than you think might be necessary. Egg whites are bland and need a well-seasoned filling to make them pop. In fact, if you can spare an egg white, taste the filling against it and re-season, if necessary.

HOW TO MAKE PERFECT HARD-BOILED EGGS

J. Kenji López-Alt, the managing culinary director at the awesome food blog *Serious Eats,* did an exhaustive exploration of how best to boil eggs a few years ago; he proved that eggs peel much easier when they are cooked the entire time in boiling water. Here is the method I use for perfect hard-boiled eggs:

Using a slotted spoon, lower the eggs into a saucepan of boiling water that's large enough to hold the eggs in a single layer. Set the timer for 10 minutes, and when it goes off, drain the eggs. Return the eggs to the saucepan, cover with ice water and let cool. Then peel.

HOW TO TRANSPORT DEVILED EGGS

1. For the minimalist cook: Set the assembled eggs in the cups of a muffin tin or in ice cube trays and cover them loosely with plastic. This option is best if you're not concerned about perfection, you're not going far, and you plan to eat the eggs as soon as you get to the party.

2. For the egg-obsessed: If you're the one who always brings the eggs, it might be worth spending the $10 to $20 for a deviled egg carrier, which you can repurpose to hold kitchen odds and ends when it's not in use.

3. For the perfectionist foodie: Bring the egg whites in an airtight container (you can stack them) and the filling in a resealable plastic bag. At the party, arrange the egg whites on a platter, snip off one of the bag corners, and use that bag to pipe the filling into the egg cavities.

WINTER

SMOKY DEVILED EGGS WITH TOASTED ROSEMARY

VEGETARIAN; GLUTEN-FREE /
MAKES 2 DOZEN DEVILED EGGS

Smoked paprika and rosemary remind me of fireplaces and Christmas trees—two signs of winter where I live in the Northeast.

2 TABLESPOONS EXTRA-VIRGIN OLIVE OIL

48 FRESH ROSEMARY LEAVES
(PULLED FROM THE STEMS)

12 PEELED HARD-BOILED LARGE EGGS

¼ CUP PLUS 2 TABLESPOONS
MAYONNAISE

1 TABLESPOON PLUS 1 TEASPOON
DIJON MUSTARD

2 TEASPOONS LEMON JUICE

½ TEASPOON SMOKED PAPRIKA

KOSHER SALT AND FRESHLY GROUND
BLACK PEPPER

Arrange a double layer of paper towels next to the stove. In a small skillet, heat the olive oil. Add the rosemary and fry, stirring frequently, for about 30 seconds. Using a slotted spoon, spread the rosemary leaves out in a single layer on the paper towels to drain.

(RECIPE CONTINUES)

Halve the hard-boiled eggs lengthwise and use a teaspoon to pop out the yolks into a mini food processor or a bowl (press them through a sieve or use a fork to mash). Add the mayonnaise, mustard, lemon juice, and smoked paprika and process or stir to combine. Season the filling generously with salt and a little pepper.

Arrange the egg white halves on a platter and spoon or pipe the filling into the whites. Top the eggs with the fried rosemary and serve.

POTLUCK PREP. The egg whites and filling can be refrigerated separately overnight. The fried rosemary can stand at room temperature on a paper towel–lined plate, loosely covered with plastic wrap, overnight.

SPRING
GREEN DEVILED EGGS AND HAM
GLUTEN-FREE / MAKES 2 DOZEN DEVILED EGGS

A quick mash of peas with lemon zest and tarragon just tastes like spring. Blended into the egg yolks, it gives the eggs a jade hue. The ham? Well, that gets crisped in the oven and served on top. These are admittedly a little fussier than the usual deviled eggs, but the effort is well worth it.

4 THIN SLICES PROSCIUTTO OR
   SERRANO HAM

4 OUNCES FROZEN PEAS (1 CUP)

2 TABLESPOONS WATER

1 TABLESPOON UNSALTED BUTTER

¼ CUP PLUS 2 TABLESPOONS MAYONNAISE

ZEST OF 1 SMALL LEMON

12 PEELED HARD-BOILED LARGE EGGS

1 TABLESPOON FINELY CHOPPED FRESH
   TARRAGON

KOSHER SALT AND FRESHLY GROUND
   BLACK PEPPER

Preheat the oven to 375°F. Line a baking sheet with parchment paper. Arrange the slices of prosciutto so they're flat on the baking sheet and bake for about 10 minutes, until darkened. Transfer the ham to a rack and let cool and become crisp; break into small pieces.

In a small pot, cook the peas with the water over medium-high heat until just heated through, about 3 minutes. Drain off any excess liquid and transfer to a bowl. Add the butter and, using a fork, mash the peas until the butter is melted and the peas have become a coarse puree. Mash in the mayonnaise and lemon zest.

Halve the eggs. Use a teaspoon to pop out the egg yolks and add them to the pea mixture. Mash the yolks with the peas until well incorporated. (To make a less coarse filling, you can mix all of it together in a mini food processor or press the yolks through a sieve.) Mix in the tarragon and season the filling generously with salt and a little pepper.

Arrange the egg whites on a platter. Spoon or pipe the filling into the egg whites, garnish with the ham crisps, and serve.

POTLUCK PREP. The egg whites and filling can be refrigerated separately overnight. The ham crisps can be kept in a resealable plastic bag overnight.

bloody mary deviled eggs

green deviled eggs and ham

green deviled eggs and ham

mustard-cornichon deviled eggs

BLOODY MARY DEVILED EGGS

GLUTEN-FREE / MAKES 2 DOZEN
DEVILED EGGS

With the tomato paste, Worcestershire sauce, and horseradish, it's remarkable how much these taste like the brunch drink. Because people's Bloody Mary preferences vary widely, I've given you lots of options for seasoning to taste. I like to garnish these with celery leaves, but if you prefer, top them with olives or slices of dill pickle.

12 PEELED HARD-BOILED LARGE EGGS

¼ CUP PLUS 2 TABLESPOONS
MAYONNAISE

3 TABLESPOONS TOMATO PASTE

1 TABLESPOON LEMON JUICE, PLUS
MORE TO TASTE

1 TEASPOON WORCESTERSHIRE SAUCE
(USE GLUTEN-FREE), PLUS MORE TO
TASTE

1 TEASPOON OLD BAY SEASONING,
PLUS MORE TO TASTE

1 TEASPOON PREPARED HORSERADISH,
PLUS MORE TO TASTE

KOSHER SALT AND FRESHLY GROUND
BLACK PEPPER

SMALL PINCH OF CAYENNE PEPPER
(OPTIONAL)

24 CELERY LEAVES OR THINLY SLICED
CELERY PIECES, FOR GARNISH

Halve the eggs lengthwise. Use a teaspoon to pop out the egg yolks into a food processor or bowl. Blend in the mayonnaise, tomato paste, lemon juice, Worcestershire, Old Bay, and horseradish. Season generously with salt and pepper, along with the cayenne if you want more heat. Add more lemon juice, Worcestershire, Old Bay, and/or horseradish, as desired.

Arrange the egg whites on a platter. Spoon or pipe the filling into the egg whites, garnish with the celery leaves, and serve.

POTLUCK PREP. The egg whites and filling can be refrigerated separately overnight.

MUSTARD-CORNICHON DEVILED EGGS

VEGETARIAN; GLUTEN-FREE /
MAKES 2 DOZEN DEVILED EGGS

Mustard and pickles are great with all things fall, from bonfires to sausages to pints of beer.

12 PEELED HARD-BOILED LARGE EGGS

¼ CUP PLUS 2 TABLESPOONS
MAYONNAISE

2 TABLESPOONS WHOLE-GRAIN
MUSTARD

6 CORNICHON PICKLES, FINELY
CHOPPED

KOSHER SALT

Halve the eggs lengthwise. Use a teaspoon to pop out the yolks and transfer to a food processor or a bowl. Mix in the mayonnaise, mustard, and cornichons. Season with salt, if necessary.

Arrange the egg whites on a platter. Spoon or pipe the filling into the whites and serve.

POTLUCK PREP. The egg whites and filling can be refrigerated separately overnight.

AQUABEET-CURED SALMON

GLUTEN-FREE / SERVES AT LEAST 8

1 (3- TO 3½-POUND) SKIN-ON SALMON FILLET, HALVED CROSSWISE

2 MEDIUM BEETS (ABOUT 1 POUND)

1 TABLESPOON FENNEL SEEDS

1 TABLESPOON GROUND CORIANDER

ZEST FROM 2 LEMONS, REMOVED WITH A VEGETABLE PEELER

1 CUP KOSHER SALT

1 CUP SUGAR

8 DROPS ANGOSTURA BITTERS (OPTIONAL)

¼ CUP AQUAVIT OR GIN

Thanks to Noma, that near mythical restaurant in Copenhagen often considered "the best in the world," we're all a little Scandinavian-food obsessed. A staple in that part of the world is gravlax—salt-and-sugar-cured salmon that is especially delicious at brunch or for cocktail parties. It also scores high on the easy-to-impress scale, with prep time taking all of 20 minutes. The beets in the cure here add a subtle flavor, but they are really there for color, creating a gorgeous fuchsia ribbon around the slices of salmon. If you don't like beets, just leave them out and grind the spices in a spice grinder rather than in the food processor.

POTLUCK PREP. Large pieces of cured salmon can be covered and refrigerated for up to 5 days. Thinly sliced salmon is best fresh (eaten within an hour or two) but can be covered and refrigerated overnight.

Use clean tweezers to pull any pin bones out of the salmon fillet. Line a 9 × 13-inch glass or ceramic baking dish lengthwise with two 30-inch pieces of plastic wrap so they overlap in the center of the dish and hang over every edge of the pan. Set one of the fillet halves skin side down in the dish. Set the other fillet half on a platter.

In a food processor, pulse the beets with the fennel, coriander, and lemon zest until finely chopped, and then process to a paste. Transfer the mixture to a bowl and add the salt, sugar, and bitters, if using.

Drizzle the Aquavit over both salmon fillets and rub it in. Rub a thick layer of beet cure all over the flesh side of the salmon in the baking dish and a thin layer all over the fish on the platter. Arrange the salmon piece on the platter atop the one in the baking dish, so they're flesh-to-flesh in the dish. Loosely cover the salmon with the plastic and set a heavy plate or two on top to lightly press the fish.

Cure the salmon in the refrigerator for about 48 hours, flipping it over every 12 hours or so and draining off the excess liquid.

Unwrap the salmon and drain off any more excess liquid. Use a spoon to push off as much of the cure as possible into the plastic wrap and discard. Rinse the fillets, pat them dry with paper towels, and transfer them to a carving board. Use a sharp knife to thinly slice the cured salmon on the diagonal, avoiding the skin. Arrange on a platter and serve.

WAYS TO USE GRAVLAX

- Serve it with a bagel spread, on toasts, or with popovers or latkes.
- Add it to a quiche.
- Chop it and toss it with hot pasta and crème fraîche.
- Finely chop it to make a faux tartare; mix it with crunchy vegetables, like cucumbers and radishes, if desired.
- Make an open-faced sandwich with whole-grain German-style bread, cream cheese, gravlax, and dill.
- Add it to hearty salads.

BUTTERY WHOLE WHEAT CRACKERS

VEGETARIAN / MAKES AT LEAST 8 DOZEN 1½-INCH CRACKERS
OR 4 DOZEN 3-INCH CRACKERS

1 CUP WHOLE WHEAT FLOUR

1 CUP ALL-PURPOSE FLOUR

¾ TEASPOON KOSHER SALT

5 TABLESPOONS UNSALTED
BUTTER, CUT INTO ½-INCH
CUBES

½ TO ¾ CUP BUTTERMILK

FLAKY SALT, FOR
SPRINKLING

I hadn't paid much attention to crackers until after my daughter—a carb-loving little monster—started eating them by the handful. I tasted several brands before settling on my favorite: Sheridan's Irish Brown Bread Crackers. I love their simple ingredient list and the fact that they taste like savory shortbread.

This is my homage to those crackers.

POTLUCK PREP. The dough can be refrigerated for up to 3 days, or wrapped tightly in plastic and frozen for up to 1 month. The crackers can be kept crisp in an airtight container for up to 5 days.

Preheat the oven to 450°F. Line 2 baking sheets with parchment paper or Silpat liners.

In a bowl, whisk the flours with the salt. Add the butter and, using a pastry blender or your fingers, work it into the flour until evenly incorporated. Add ½ cup of the buttermilk and stir until evenly moistened. If you have a lot of dry crumbs (this will depend on your whole wheat flour), add up to ¼ cup more of buttermilk, a little at a time. If the dough ends up feeling sticky, it's okay; just generously flour it while rolling it out.

Transfer the dough to a floured work surface and knead lightly just to combine. Divide the dough into 4 pieces, cover, and refrigerate for at least 20 minutes.

Flour a rolling pin. On the floured work surface, press one piece of dough into a square. Roll it out into a 6 x 9-inch rectangle, about 1/16 inch thick, moving it occasionally to keep it from sticking. Use a fork to poke holes all over the dough. Using a pizza cutter or pastry wheel, trim any ragged edges, then cut the dough into squares. Sprinkle the squares with flaky salt, and then transfer them to one of the prepared baking sheets. Roll and cut the remaining dough pieces, transferring the squares to the baking sheets.

Bake the crackers for 7 to 9 minutes, until golden but dark brown in spots. Transfer the crackers to a rack and let cool completely. They will become darker and crisper as they cool.

SRIRACHA "PIMIENTO" CHEESE

VEGETARIAN; GLUTEN-FREE (EXCEPT FOR THE CRACKERS, FOR SERVING) /
MAKES ABOUT 3 CUPS

1 CUP MAYONNAISE (I'M A HELLMANN'S GIRL, BUT USE WHAT YOU PREFER)

¼ CUP FINELY CHOPPED SWEET ONION

1 TEASPOON SRIRACHA, PLUS MORE FOR SEASONING

1 POUND SHARP CHEDDAR CHEESE, COARSELY SHREDDED (ABOUT 5 LOOSELY PACKED CUPS)

½ CUP FINELY CHOPPED PEPPADEW PEPPERS (ABOUT 8) OR PIMIENTOS, PLUS MORE FOR GARNISH

CRISP VEGETABLES OR CRACKERS (RITZ ARE CLASSIC), FOR SERVING

In the U.S. South, pimiento cheese is so popular you can buy it at the gas station. Over the last decade or so, cooks beyond the area have adopted this regional classic as their own, and for good reason: Southerners know how to make great party food. This recipe is adapted from one by Angie Mosier, an Atlanta-based food writer, photographer, and stylist. I spiced up her version with Sriracha instead of cayenne, and use sweet pickled Peppadew peppers instead of pimientos, which add terrific vinegary tang.

In a food processor, blend the mayonnaise with the onion and Sriracha. Add the cheese and pulse until finely chopped. Add the peppers and pulse to combine.

Scrape the pimiento cheese into a resealable container or a bowl, and garnish with more chopped peppers. Refrigerate for at least 1 hour before serving with vegetables or crackers.

POTLUCK PREP. You can refrigerate this for up to 3 days.

RED PEPPER, EGGPLANT, AND WALNUT DIP

VEGAN; GLUTEN-FREE (EXCEPT FOR THE PITA CHIPS, FOR SERVING) /
MAKES ABOUT 2 CUPS

1 CUP WALNUTS

ONE (8-OUNCE) EGGPLANT, PREFERABLY ITALIAN

¼ CUP EXTRA-VIRGIN OLIVE OIL, PLUS MORE FOR RUBBING AND DRIZZLING

1½ POUNDS SWEET RED PEPPERS (ABOUT 3 VERY LARGE BELL PEPPERS)

3 GARLIC CLOVES

¼ CUP SMOKED ALMONDS OR ROASTED SALTED ALMONDS WITH A PINCH OF SMOKED PAPRIKA

3 TABLESPOONS FRESH LEMON JUICE

1 TEASPOON POMEGRANATE MOLASSES (OPTIONAL)

KOSHER SALT AND FRESHLY GROUND BLACK PEPPER

CHOPPED FRESH FLAT-LEAF PARSLEY LEAVES, FOR GARNISH

CRISP VEGETABLES OR PITA CHIPS, FOR SERVING

Many countries have a silky, luscious red pepper dip or spread—bold, nutty romesco in Spain; garlicky, eggplant-enriched ajvaar in Serbia; and pomegranate molasses–sweetened muhammara in Syria and other parts of the Middle East. I combined my favorite parts of all of them to create a dip that's smoky, tangy, sweet, and deeply flavored. It's hearty but not overwhelmingly rich. I particularly love using the long varieties of sweet red peppers in this dip because I find the flavors more interesting, but red bell peppers work just fine, too.

Preheat a toaster oven or regular oven to 350°F. Spread the walnuts on a baking sheet or piece of foil and toast for about 5 minutes, until golden and fragrant. Transfer to a food processor and let cool until warm.

Meanwhile, turn the broiler to high and line a rimmed baking sheet with foil.

Pierce the eggplant all over with a fork and rub the eggplant and peppers with a thin coating of olive oil. Transfer to the prepared baking sheet and broil on high, about 4 inches from the heat, turning occasionally, until the peppers are blackened all over and the eggplant is dark and very soft, about 20 minutes. Transfer to a work surface and let cool until cool enough to handle. (You can blacken the peppers and eggplant on the grill as well.)

Rub the garlic cloves with a little olive oil and broil, turning once, until blistered and softened, 2 to 3 minutes per side. (You can skewer them to do this on the grill.) Transfer to a food processor.

Stem and seed the peppers and rub off the skin; transfer the flesh to a food processor. Peel and stem the eggplant and add the flesh to the food processor. Add the walnuts, the almonds, lemon juice, and pomegranate molasses and process to a coarse puree. With the machine on, add the ¼ cup olive oil in a thin stream and process until creamy. Season to taste with salt and pepper.

Scrape the dip into a serving bowl and drizzle with a bit more olive oil. Garnish with the parsley and serve with vegetables and pita chips.

POTLUCK PREP. The dip can be refrigerated for up to 2 days, and in fact, the flavors are even better after they have a day to meld.

INDIAN-SPICED SPINACH-YOGURT DIP

VEGETARIAN; GLUTEN-FREE (EXCEPT FOR THE PITA CHIPS, FOR SERVING) /
MAKES ABOUT 2½ CUPS

1 POUND FRESH SPINACH (NOT BABY SPINACH), THICK STEMS TRIMMED AND CLEANED WELL

1 TABLESPOON GRAPESEED OR OTHER NEUTRAL OIL

3 GARLIC CLOVES, MINCED

1 (2-INCH) PIECE FRESH GINGER, PEELED AND MINCED

2 SMALL JALAPEÑOS, STEMMED, SEEDED, AND MINCED

KOSHER SALT

2 CUPS PLAIN GREEK YOGURT (I LIKE 2%)

2 TABLESPOONS FRESH LEMON JUICE, PLUS MORE TO TASTE

½ TEASPOON GARAM MASALA, PLUS MORE TO TASTE (SEE NOTE)

FRESHLY GROUND BLACK PEPPER

PITA CHIPS OR CRISP VEGETABLES, FOR SERVING

Ever since I was a little girl, my aunt has made a creamy spinach dip, served in a bread bowl. It's a classic recipe pulled from the package of Knorr Vegetable Recipe Mix. This dip is reminiscent of the classic but is inspired by one of my favorite Indian take-out dishes, saag paneer. If you don't have a food processor, you can finely chop the cooked spinach and stir everything else together in a large bowl.

NOTE. Garam masala is a blend of some sweeter spices, like cinnamon, cardamom, cloves, and nutmeg, along with cumin, coriander, and black pepper. It is not always easy to find. To substitute, you could use a small pinch of some of these spices that you have on hand. You could also add curry powder, which won't have the same flavor but it will still be tasty.

In a large, deep skillet, heat 1 inch of water and season generously with salt. Add the spinach, cover, and cook until wilted (stirring a few times if necessary), about 3 minutes. Drain in a colander and cool under cold running water, then squeeze out any excess liquid. Transfer the spinach to a food processor.

Wipe out the skillet and heat the oil. Add the garlic, ginger, jalapeños, and a large pinch of salt and cook over medium-high heat, stirring, until the garlic is just starting to brown, about 2 minutes. Scrape everything into the food processor.

Pulse the spinach in the food processor until finely chopped. Add the yogurt, lemon juice, and garam masala and pulse just to combine. Season generously with salt and pepper, adding more lemon juice and garam masala, if desired, and then serve with pita chips and vegetables.

POTLUCK PREP. The dip can be refrigerated for up to 3 days. Serve chilled.

THE NEW CRUDITÉS

With farmers' markets brimming with alt-hued carrots and lesser-known vegetables, it's time to rethink the crudités platter. Instead of the vegetables being an afterthought, make them an integral part of your dip presentation. Choose two or three in-season vegetables and prep them with care. Let this list inspire you. (See more photographs on pages 20–21.)

ASPARAGUS. You don't often see asparagus as part of a crudités platter, but they're a great option in the spring for dips that aren't too stiff. Blanch them according to the instructions on page 40.

BELGIAN ENDIVE. These slightly bitter, crisp-juicy leaves are great with creamy or pungent dips (like the Sriracha "Pimiento" Cheese, page 33, and the Smoked Fish–Onion Dip, page 41). Plus, prep is a breeze: just pull the leaves from the bulbs and arrange them nicely on the platter.

BROCCOLI, CAULIFLOWER, AND THE LIKE. I prefer to blanch broccoli, cauliflower, and its cousin romanesco (see instructions on page 40) because the salted liquid seasons them from the inside out; they're also easier to digest this way. While broccoli and cauliflower are available year-round, they're especially sweet from fall to spring.

CARROTS. Look for real baby carrots (the ones that are actually pulled from the ground early) at farmers' markets or stores like Whole Foods. You can serve them whole, with pieces of the tops still attached. Even better, markets are now stocking carrots in a rainbow of colors. Give them a quick scrub and cut them into sticks if they're thick.

CELERY. Celery may feel a little ho-hum these days, but that slightly salty snap is just the right thing with many dips. (Not to mention that farmers' market celery—available when the weather is cool—tastes so much more intense than the supermarket variety, it seems like a different vegetable.) For a prettier presentation, serve spears with the leaves on. A quick ice-water soak (instructions on page 40) will make them extra crisp.

CUCUMBER. Instead of the huge, waxed cucumbers, which almost always need to be peeled, I love to serve small cucumbers, like the Persian variety, and cut them into spears. If the mini cukes aren't available, look for English cucumbers (seedless), which are usually wrapped in plastic to protect their thin skins. Just slice these into rounds, arrange on a platter, and serve. Cucumbers are available year-round, but summer is when you'll find them at the farmers' market. If they feel limp at all, soak them whole in ice water to refresh them (instructions on page 40).

FENNEL. The crisp texture of fennel is as satisfying as potato chips, and its anise flavor makes it a great pre- or post-meal *digestif.* Fennel bulbs admittedly look daunting, but with a little practice (and a sharp knife), you can slice one in 30 seconds flat. Here's how to do it: Remove the stalks with the fronds. Stand the bulb vertically with the root end down and halve it lengthwise. Set the halves with the flat sides down and halve those so you have quarters. Cut out the core and the tough part of the root end, then slice into vertical strips. If you prefer something more exotic looking, you can also slice your halved fennel bulb crosswise so you get horseshoe-shaped pieces. Fennel is available year-round, but it tends to be best in the cooler months. If it gets a little limp in the fridge, refresh with an ice-water bath (instructions on page 40).

GREEN BEANS AND THE LIKE. When they're incredibly fresh, summer beans—including green beans, wax beans, and flat romano beans—are delicious raw. The best way to know if they are fresh? Taste them. If they're sweet and crisp, just throw them on the platter, raw. If they're even the slightest bit tough, blanch them according to the instructions on page 40.

PEPPERS. Bell peppers work best for crudités because they're especially crisp and have enough flesh for dipping. Just slice off the flesh vertically from around the stem, remove the seeds and ribs, and then cut into strips.

POTATOES. Halved roasted or boiled fingerling potatoes are awesome with creamy dips. To roast, preheat the oven to 400°F. Toss the halved fingerling potatoes with extra-virgin olive oil and season with salt and pepper. Arrange them on a baking sheet, cut sides down, and roast for about 20 minutes, until browned and tender. To boil them instead, cook them whole until tender, about 10 minutes; let them cool and then halve them.

RADISHES. These cool-weather vegetables are gorgeous on a crudités platter. I usually like to leave the finger-like French Breakfast radishes (and other small, long varieties) whole, with some greens attached. Your standard red radishes are usually best halved or quartered. Other radishes, like the stunning watermelon radish, are generally best halved and thinly sliced. To make them extra crisp, soak them in ice water (instructions follow).

SNOW PEAS AND SUGAR-SNAP PEAS. While both of these early summer peas can be great raw, I usually prefer them with a quick blanch (instructions at right). Before you cook them, bite into one. If it's fibrous, the peas will likely need to be stringed. Just pull on the stem end of each pea to pull off the strings that run along the side.

SUMMER SQUASH AND ZUCCHINI. When summer squash is especially fresh, raw rounds or spears of it can be a great option for dipping. For the best-flavored squash to eat raw, stick with the long varieties and select medium ones with few to no blemishes.

SUNCHOKES (JERUSALEM ARTICHOKES). These sunflower tubers look like pieces of fresh ginger but they have the texture of jícama and a delicious sweet, slightly nutty flavor. But here's the thing—this vegetable is packed with inulin, the stuff that's often added to fiber bars. If I don't know my guests well, I probably wouldn't serve them. Otherwise, I would put out a few, perhaps with a sign, "Crunchy and sweet but may cause digestive excitement." Don't be daunted by the shape: you don't have to peel them; just give them a scrub, and then slice them lengthwise into pieces about ¼ inch thick.

TREVISO. This bitter leafy vegetable is an adventurous choice and is not always easy to find. Like Belgian endive, treviso has leaves with firm, scoopable bottoms. To serve, just pull the leaves from the heads.

TURNIPS. Freshly harvested turnips can be spectacular raw. I especially love the small, snowy white Japanese harukei turnips. The flavor is so mild that you can just quarter them like radishes to serve with your dip. If desired, crisp up the turnips in ice water (instructions are below).

BLANCHING AND SHOCKING TOUGH VEGETABLES

This method turns tough veggies into crisp-tender snacks while seasoning them from the inside out. Here's how to do it:

1. Set a bowl of ice water next to the stove. This will be used to quickly stop the cooking.

2. Bring a pot of water to a boil that's large enough to hold the vegetables you're going to blanch. Season the water generously with salt. Add the vegetables to the water and cook until crisp-tender, usually just a minute or two, but it will depend on the size of the vegetable. Drain the veggies in a strainer or colander, and immediately plunge them into the ice water to cool. Remove them and drain them well and shake or pat dry.

Most blanched and shocked vegetables will stay tasty for a couple of days in the fridge; the exceptions are cauliflower and broccoli, which are usually best the day they're cooked.

ICE-WATER BATH FOR CRISP VEGETABLES

If carrots, radishes, cucumbers, turnips, celery, fennel, and other crisp, firm-fleshed vegetables are ever feeling a little limp or spongy, you can refresh them in an ice-water bath.

1. Fill a large bowl with ice water. Add the vegetables (cucumbers should be whole but others can be whole or sliced) and let stand for about 15 minutes, until refreshed.

2. Drain and pat dry.

SMOKED FISH–ONION DIP

GLUTEN-FREE / MAKES ABOUT 2 CUPS

- 2 TABLESPOONS UNSALTED BUTTER
- 2 SMALL ONIONS, FINELY CHOPPED (ABOUT 1¼ CUPS)
- ½ CUP SOUR CREAM
- 1 (7-OUNCE) CONTAINER PLAIN GREEK YOGURT (PREFERABLY 2%)
- ½ TEASPOON WORCESTERSHIRE SAUCE (CONFIRM THAT IT'S GLUTEN-FREE)
- 3 OUNCES SMOKED BLUEFISH, MACKEREL, TROUT, OR HOT-SMOKED SALMON, SKIN REMOVED
- KOSHER SALT AND FRESHLY GROUND BLACK PEPPER
- CAYENNE PEPPER
- CHOPPED FRESH FLAT-LEAF PARSLEY, FOR GARNISH

This dip, which is a cross between two retro appetizers—onion dip and smoked fish pâté—is my go-to when I can find smoked bluefish at the farmers' market. Granted, the recipe works with any hot-smoked fish, so use what you can find. Blue potato chips are a stunning accompaniment, as are crisp vegetables, like radishes and fennel.

In a medium skillet set over medium heat, melt the butter. Add the onions and cook, stirring occasionally, until soft, about 8 minutes. Increase the heat to medium-high; as some of the onions brown and the pan seems like it might start to burn, add a teaspoon or so of water. Continue cooking, stirring, and adding a little water as necessary, until the onions are very soft and very browned and all of the liquid has evaporated, about 10 minutes longer. Let the onions cool to warm, about 15 minutes.

In a medium bowl, combine the onions, the sour cream, yogurt, and Worcestershire sauce. Gently fold in the fish and season the dip with salt, black pepper, and cayenne to taste. Garnish with parsley and serve chilled.

POTLUCK PREP. The dip can be refrigerated for up to 2 days and can stand at room temperature for up to 2½ hours.

RADISHES
WITH SEAWEED-SESAME BUTTER AND SMOKED SALT

VEGETARIAN (OPTIONAL); GLUTEN-FREE / SERVES 8 TO 12

½ CUP (1 STICK) UNSALTED BUTTER, AT ROOM TEMPERATURE

1 TABLESPOON JAPANESE FURIKAKE SEASONING (SEE NOTE)

3 DOZEN FRENCH BREAKFAST RADISHES OR STANDARD RED RADISHES (ABOUT 4 BUNCHES), LEAVES TRIMMED AS DESIRED, RADISHES HALVED IF LARGE

SMOKED SALT OR OTHER FLAKY SALT

The combination of crisp, peppery radishes with sweet fat and a sprinkle of flaky salt is just perfection. Yet, I couldn't help but mess with the combination (a little). Blending the butter with Japanese furikake seasoning and adding smoked salt makes it extra savory.

Furikake seasonings can vary depending on the brand, but for the most part, they always contain bonito flakes, which are derived from fish, and some also contain MSG. Because both ingredients might be controversial, I've offered a vegetarian, MSG-free version you can make yourself.

In a mixing bowl, sprinkle the butter with the furikake and use a small spatula to blend it together. Transfer the butter to a ramekin or small serving bowl.

Arrange the radishes on a platter. Set out the butter with a small knife for spreading and a small bowl of smoked salt for sprinkling or dipping.

POTLUCK PREP. You can prepare the furikake butter and refrigerate it for several days. Bring it to room temperature before serving. For extra-crisp radishes, soak them in ice water for about 30 minutes. Dry well before serving.

NOTE. To make about 1 tablespoon vegetarian furikake-like seasoning, use tongs to wave ¼ sheet of nori over a medium burner for 1 to 2 seconds, until it becomes brittle. Transfer to a spice grinder or mini food processor and grind or pulse until finely chopped. Transfer to a small bowl. In a small dry skillet, toast 1½ teaspoons sesame seeds, shaking occasionally, until they start to pop; let cool. Transfer the seeds to the bowl, add a pinch of sugar, and toss. (Alternatively, you can use 1½ teaspoons nori flakes and 1½ teaspoons pretoasted sesame seeds.)

ROASTED CARROT AND CURRY HUMMUS
WITH LIME

VEGAN; GLUTEN-FREE / MAKES ABOUT 4 CUPS

½ POUND DRIED CHICKPEAS
(ABOUT 1 GENEROUS CUP)

1 TABLESPOON BAKING SODA

½ POUND CARROTS,
SCRUBBED AND CUT INTO
1-INCH PIECES

6 GARLIC CLOVES, UNPEELED

¼ CUP PLUS 2 TABLESPOONS
EXTRA-VIRGIN OLIVE
OIL, PLUS MORE FOR
DRIZZLING

1 TABLESPOON MADRAS
CURRY POWDER

¼ CUP WELL-STIRRED TAHINI

¼ CUP PLUS 2 TABLESPOONS
FRESH LIME JUICE

KOSHER SALT AND FRESHLY
GROUND BLACK PEPPER

CHOPPED FRESH CILANTRO
AND TOASTED PUMPKIN
SEEDS, FOR GARNISH

Here's a variation on hummus that's so far from traditional that I debated whether to even call it hummus. But because the dip contains chickpeas, garlic, and tahini, I figured it was okay.

I promise that soaking and cooking dried chickpeas is worth the effort, because it results in a super-smooth dip. If you can't spare the time it takes to prep them, substitute 3 cups of canned chickpeas (from two 15-ounce cans) and simmer them until very soft, about 20 minutes, then drain and reserve the cooking water. Serve with pita chips (which are usually not gluten-free), rice crackers, or vegetables.

POTLUCK PREP. The hummus can be refrigerated in an airtight container for up to 3 days. Bring it to room temperature and garnish it before serving.

In a bowl, cover the chickpeas with 2 inches of water and stir in the baking soda. Refrigerate for 8 hours or overnight. Drain and rinse.

Preheat the oven to 400°F.

In a large saucepan, cover the rinsed chickpeas with 2 inches of water and bring to a boil. Reduce the heat and simmer over medium-low heat until the chickpeas are very tender and starting to fall apart, 30 to 40 minutes or even longer, depending on the freshness of the chickpeas. Drain, reserving 1 cup of the cooking water.

Meanwhile, on a small baking sheet, toss the carrots and the garlic with 2 tablespoons of the olive oil, 1½ teaspoons of the curry powder, and season with salt and pepper. Roast for about 30 minutes, until the carrots and garlic are quite browned and tender.

When the garlic is cool, squeeze the cloves into a food processor. Add the carrots, chickpeas, ½ cup of the cooking liquid, ¼ cup of the olive oil, the remaining 1½ teaspoons curry powder, the tahini, and lime juice. Process until creamy, adding more cooking liquid if you'd like a looser hummus. Season with salt and pepper.

Transfer to a serving bowl. Using a spoon, make a swirl. Drizzle in some olive oil, garnish with the cilantro and pumpkin seeds, and serve.

LENTIL AND PECAN PÂTÉ

VEGAN / MAKES ABOUT 3 CUPS

½ CUP EXTRA-VIRGIN OLIVE OIL

1 MEDIUM ONION, FINELY CHOPPED

KOSHER SALT AND FRESHLY GROUND PEPPER

1 CUP BROWN LENTILS

3½ CUPS WATER

1½ CUPS WHOLE SHELLED PECANS (ABOUT 6 OUNCES)

2 TABLESPOONS LOW-SODIUM SOY SAUCE

1 TABLESPOON MISO, PREFERABLY WHITE

2 TABLESPOONS BALSAMIC VINEGAR

CRACKERS OR TOASTS, FOR SERVING

I've been intrigued with meatless pâté ever since trying the Faux Gras sold by a small company called The Regal Vegan (theregalvegan.com). With a combination of lentils, nuts, and umami-rich flavorings, they have managed to create an incredibly rich and savory spread. This is my vegan pâté; it isn't quite as decadent as true foie gras, which is made with tons of animal fat, but that can be a good thing: you can eat a lot of this without needing a nap afterward. Serve this pâté as you would any other, with crackers and, perhaps, fig jam or pickles.

POTLUCK PREP. The pâté can be refrigerated in an airtight container for up to 5 days.

Preheat a toaster oven or regular oven to 350°F.

In a medium saucepan, heat 2 tablespoons of the olive oil over low heat. Add the onion and ½ teaspoon salt; cover and cook until softened, about 10 minutes. Uncover, increase the heat to medium, and cook until golden, about 10 more minutes. Add the lentils and water and bring to a boil. Simmer, partly covered and stirring occasionally, until the lentils are very tender and starting to fall apart, about 30 minutes. Drain the lentils, reserving any cooking liquid in a liquid measuring cup, and transfer to a food processor; let cool slightly.

Meanwhile, spread the pecans out on a baking sheet and toast for about 5 minutes, until fragrant and slightly darkened. Transfer to the food processor and let cool slightly.

Add the soy sauce, miso, and balsamic vinegar to the food processor and pulse until the lentils and pecans are finely chopped and starting to form a paste. With the machine on, add the remaining ¼ cup plus 2 tablespoons olive oil and process to a paste. If you want to loosen the consistency of the pâté, add some of the cooking liquid, 1 tablespoon at a time, and process between additions. Season the pâté with more salt and some pepper, if desired, and serve with crackers or toasts.

HARISSA-ROASTED CHICKPEAS

VEGAN; GLUTEN-FREE / MAKES ABOUT 2 CUPS

2 (15½-OUNCE) CANS CHICKPEAS, DRAINED

1 TABLESPOON EXTRA-VIRGIN OLIVE OIL

1 TABLESPOON HARISSA

KOSHER SALT

CAYENNE PEPPER OR FRESHLY GROUND BLACK PEPPER (OPTIONAL)

Harissa is a spicy North African paste made with chiles and spices, and it's becoming more widely available at specialty markets and Mediterranean grocery stores. The paste adds a ton of flavor to these roasted chickpeas, which are an easy and healthy snack to pull together for a potluck. Because the size of chickpeas can vary, you may need to adjust the cooking time. The goal is to have chickpeas that are mostly crunchy, but not blackened. Also, since the heat level of harissa can differ from one brand to the next, you might find you want to add more spice before serving.

Line a baking sheet with parchment paper. Spread the chickpeas out on the baking sheet and put them in the oven while you preheat it to 400°F (this helps to get them nice and dry).

In a large bowl, whisk the olive oil with the harissa. Add the dry chickpeas and toss; season generously with salt (at least ½ teaspoon). Return the chickpeas to the baking sheet.

Roast for 40 to 50 minutes, shaking the pan every 15 minutes or so, until browned and crisp. Let the chickpeas cool completely on the baking sheet. Transfer to a bowl, season with more salt and the cayenne or black pepper, if desired, and serve.

POTLUCK PREP. The chickpeas can be kept in an airtight container at room temperature for up to 2 days.

WATERMELON AGUA FRESCA

VEGAN; GLUTEN-FREE / MAKES ABOUT 6 DRINKS

6 CUPS CHOPPED SEEDLESS
   WATERMELON (ABOUT
   2 POUNDS)

3 TABLESPOONS FRESH
   LIME JUICE

¼ CUP SUGAR

16 TO 20 DROPS ANGOSTURA
   BITTERS

1½ CUPS CLUB SODA, CHILLED

1 CUP ICE CUBES

1 LIME, THINLY SLICED,
   FOR SERVING

This boozeless drink tastes just a little bit grown-up, thanks to the addition of Angostura bitters, which you can eliminate if that's not your thing. I like to use pre-cut watermelon so the drink comes together quickly. For a large party, you can serve this in a punch bowl or wide-mouthed canister with a ladle.

In a blender or food processor, puree the watermelon. Strain the juice through a sieve into a pitcher. Add the lime juice, sugar, and bitters and stir with a long-handled spoon until the sugar is dissolved. Refrigerate for at least 1 hour.

Add the club soda, ice cubes, and sliced lime to the agua fresca and serve.

POTLUCK PREP. The agua fresca base can be refrigerated for up to 2 days. Add the club soda, ice cubes, and sliced lime just before serving.

~

ELDERFLOWER AND SPARKLING WINE COCKTAIL
WITH MEYER LEMON AND MINT

VEGAN; GLUTEN-FREE / MAKES 6 DRINKS

6 TABLESPOONS FRESH
MEYER LEMON JUICE

6 TABLESPOONS
ELDERFLOWER
CONCENTRATE
(ALSO KNOWN AS
ELDERFLOWER SYRUP) OR
ELDERFLOWER LIQUEUR

6 SMALL FRESH MINT SPRIGS

1 (750-ML) BOTTLE DRY
SPARKLING WINE, WELL
CHILLED

This lovely drink is essentially a lighter, more floral French 75. To keep the drink less boozy, I prefer to add elderflower concentrate, which you can buy at IKEA or from gourmetpantry.com, but you can also add elderflower liqueur, such as St-Germaine.

In a small pitcher or liquid measuring cup, combine the lemon juice and elderflower concentrate. Pour 1 ounce (2 tablespoons) of the mixture into each of 6 Champagne flutes. Add a mint sprig to each glass, top with the sparkling wine, and serve.

POTLUCK PREP. The elderflower–lemon juice mixture can be refrigerated for up to 2 days.

APPLE-GINGER-BOURBON COCKTAIL

VEGAN; GLUTEN-FREE / MAKES 8 DRINKS

2½ INCHES FRESH GINGER, SLICED INTO ROUNDS

1 CUP WATER

1 QUART APPLE CIDER

1½ CUPS BOURBON

1 CUP FRESH LEMON JUICE

ICE CUBES

This spicy drink, which you can serve hot or cold, screams "fall." Thanks to the lemon, ginger, and bourbon, it also makes an excellent cold remedy. Or, at least you can tell your friends that.

In a medium saucepan, combine the ginger slices with the water and bring to a boil. Remove from the heat and let cool to room temperature. Strain the ginger water into a 2-quart pitcher.

Add the apple cider, bourbon, and lemon juice to the ginger water and stir. Refrigerate for at least 1 hour, until well chilled. Serve in ice-filled glasses.

POTLUCK PREP. This cocktail can be blended and refrigerated for up to 2 days.

VARIATION. Instead of chilling the cocktail mixture, you can heat it in a saucepan, transfer it to a Thermos bottle, and serve it hot. Or serve it from a slow cooker with a ladle!

RIESLING PUNCH
WITH GIN, CUCUMBER, AND LIME

VEGAN; GLUTEN-FREE / MAKES 4 TO 6 DRINKS

1 (750-ML) BOTTLE DRY RIESLING

¼ CUP GIN

¼ CUP SIMPLE SYRUP (SEE NOTE)

1 LIME, THINLY SLICED

1 SMALL CUCUMBER (2 TO 3 OUNCES), THINLY SLICED

This pitcher drink is immensely refreshing and easy to make, with no citrus squeezing required. For a crowd, you can easily double or triple the quantities and serve it in a punch bowl or one of those multi-gallon drink canisters.

In a large pitcher, combine the wine, gin, simple syrup, and sliced lime and cucumber. Refrigerate until well chilled, at least 1 hour. Add 1 cup of ice cubes and serve in ice-filled glasses.

NOTE. To make simple syrup, combine ¼ cup sugar and ¼ cup water in a pot and bring to a boil over medium-high heat. Simmer, stirring occasionally, until the sugar is dissolved, 1 to 2 minutes. Let cool. The syrup will keep in the refrigerator for 1 month.

POTLUCK PREP. The Riesling, gin, and simple syrup can be combined and refrigerated for up to 2 days. Add the lime and cucumber within 4 hours of serving.

SPICED ORANGE PUNCH
WITH APEROL

GLUTEN-FREE / MAKES ABOUT 12 DRINKS

½ CUP WATER

½ CUP SUGAR

2 STAR ANISE

2 CINNAMON STICKS

1 VANILLA BEAN,
SPLIT AND SCRAPED

2 CUPS FRESH ORANGE JUICE
(FROM ABOUT 12 SMALL
ORANGES)

½ CUP FRESH LEMON JUICE
(FROM 4 TO 6 LEMONS)

1½ CUPS APEROL OR CAMPARI

1 LARGE ICE MOLD

2 (750-ML) BOTTLES DRY
SPARKLING ROSÉ WINE

1 SLICED ORANGE, FOR
SERVING

When my high school friends get together for a holiday party, someone always makes Cold Duck Punch, a headache-inducing blend of sparkling wine, juice, ginger ale, and sherbet. This is my grown-up take on that, which is less sweet and boozier. With the spiced syrup (you can vary the spices as you like), it's a lovely punch for the December holiday season.

To make an ice mold, you can freeze water in a Bundt pan or a plastic quart container. Dip the mold in warm water to loosen the ice, if necessary.

In a small saucepan, combine the water with the sugar, star anise, cinnamon, and vanilla seeds, and bring to a boil, stirring to dissolve the sugar. Turn off the heat and let stand until cool. Strain the syrup into a small pitcher or liquid measuring cup and discard the spices. Add the orange juice, lemon juice, and Aperol to the syrup and refrigerate until well chilled.

In a punch bowl, combine the juice mixture with the ice mold. Pour in the sparkling wine. Float the sliced oranges on top and serve with a ladle.

POTLUCK PREP. The spiced syrup can be refrigerated for up to 1 month. The blend of orange juice, lemon juice, Aperol, and syrup can be refrigerated for up to 5 days.

MAIN-COURSE SALADS AND OTHER ROOM-TEMPERATURE MAIN DISHES

MIDDLE EASTERN SEVEN-LAYER SALAD
WITH QUINOA

VEGETARIAN; GLUTEN-FREE / SERVES AT LEAST 10

FOR THE SALAD

- 2 CUPS QUINOA (ANY COLOR, BUT BLACK IS ESPECIALLY STUNNING), RINSED
- 5 CUPS WATER
- KOSHER SALT AND FRESHLY GROUND BLACK PEPPER
- 1 MEDIUM HEAD ICEBERG LETTUCE, CORED AND CUT INTO BITE-SIZE PIECES
- 4 CUPS FRESH HERB LEAVES, SUCH AS MINT, PARSLEY, CILANTRO, TARRAGON, AND DILL, ROUGHLY CHOPPED (THE MORE VARIETY YOU USE, THE BETTER)
- 1 BUNCH RED RADISHES (ABOUT 10), HALVED AND THINLY SLICED (ABOUT 4 CUPS)
- 1 POUND SEEDLESS CUCUMBERS, CUT INTO ½-INCH PIECES (ABOUT 4 CUPS)

FOR THE DRESSING

- ½ TEASPOON EACH CUMIN SEEDS, CORIANDER SEEDS, AND YELLOW MUSTARD SEEDS
- 2 CUPS PLAIN GREEK YOGURT (PREFERABLY FULL-FAT OR 2%)
- 1 CUP MAYONNAISE
- 2 TABLESPOONS FRESH LEMON JUICE
- 2 TABLESPOONS WHITE WINE VINEGAR
- KOSHER SALT

I love a seven-layer salad in theory, but the problem is that the bacon, sharp cheese, and raw scallions tend to over-power everything else, so you can barely taste a vegetable. Here, I take a cue from the Middle East, adding a layer of herbs, a sprinkling of toasted spices, and a yogurt dressing.

POTLUCK PREP. The salad can be refrigerated for at least 8 hours before serving and can stand at room temperature for up to 2 hours.

ASSEMBLE THE SALAD: In a large, heavy pot, cover the quinoa with the water, add 1 teaspoon salt, and bring to a boil. Cover and simmer over medium-low heat until the quinoa is tender and the water is absorbed, 18 to 20 minutes. Uncover the pot, top with a clean kitchen towel or a layer of paper towels, and close the pot again; let stand 5 minutes. (This will help ensure the quinoa is dry and fluffy.) Spread the hot quinoa out on a platter or baking sheet and let cool to room temperature. (This sounds like a fussy step, but it helps the quinoa cool without overcooking and getting mushy.)

In a very large glass or clear plastic serving bowl, spread the iceberg lettuce in a single layer and season lightly with salt and pepper. Arrange the herbs on top, followed by the quinoa. Spread the radishes on top, followed by the cucumbers, pushing them toward the edge of the bowl if you don't have enough of each vegetable to form a complete layer.

MAKE THE DRESSING: In a dry skillet, toast the spices over moderate heat until fragrant, about 1 minute. Transfer to a mortar or a bowl and let cool. Use a pestle or the bottom of an ice cream scoop to lightly crush the spices.

In a medium bowl, whisk the yogurt with the mayonnaise, lemon juice, and vinegar. Season with salt. Spread the dressing over the salad, sprinkle with the spices, and refrigerate for at least 1 hour before serving.

quinoa

barley

amaranth

ON USING WHOLE GRAINS IN SALADS

Grain salads are perfect for potlucks because they can usually be made well ahead and they don't wilt at room temperature. You can find whole-grain berries at health food stores and markets like Whole Foods. Thanks to companies like Bob's Red Mill (bobsredmill.com), many of these grains are becoming even more widely available. Here are some tips for making better grain salads, along with a quick glossary of grains and ideas for adding them to other recipes in this book.

1. Dressing attaches better to well-dried, cooked grains. To quickly dry them, spread them out on baking sheets. (This also helps to cool them faster.)

2. To get your grains to absorb the dressing well, toss them with the dressing while still slightly warm.

3. Because grains tend to drink up both salt and acid, season the salad when you make it and taste it again just before serving, adding a little salt and lemon juice or vinegar, if necessary. You'll find this is especially true if the salad spends any time in the refrigerator. (Cold food almost always needs an extra hit of seasoning.)

4. When building a salad, create a mixture of textures by using soft cooked vegetables, crisp raw ones, crunchy things like nuts, chewy things like dried fruit, and creamy, fatty cheese. Consider mixing two or more types of grains, or even grains and lentils. For best results, cook each grain separately.

5. Even if you make most of the salad ahead, add all the tender-leaved vegetables and herbs within an hour of serving.

GRAINS TO TRY AND HOW TO USE THEM

AMARANTH. People keep predicting that this tiny gluten-free seed with Aztec origins is the next quinoa. A small handful of the cooked grain adds an appealing little pop to salads, as well as a good hit of protein. Since amaranth can cook up like porridge, be sure to drain it very well. Try with Grilled Corn Salad with Lime Mayo, Cilantro, and Radishes (page 149).

BUCKWHEAT. Earthy tasting, this seed has nothing to do with wheat; in fact, it's completely gluten-free and is a member of the rhubarb family. It's especially tasty with green

farro

vegetables and mushrooms. Try with Green Things and Potato Salad (page 153) in place of the potatoes.

BARLEY. Often sold pearled (with much of the hull brushed off), barley is chewy, sweet, and mild. When I see unhulled barley at a store (a variety called Purple Prairie is especially gorgeous), I pick it up to add to salads and soups. Try with Roasted and Raw Brussels Sprouts Salad with Pecorino and Pomegranate (page 165).

FARRO, EINKORN, KAMUT, AND SPELT. These ancient wheat varieties have seen a resurgence lately because they have such great stories (einkorn, for example, is thought to go back to ancient Egyptian times). These varieties can also be easier for some people to digest. Farro is the most widely available and is usually sold pearled. Kamut is a trademarked name of khorasan wheat; when the name is used, it certifies that the strain is pure and has been grown organically. Try any of these varieties with the cauliflower salad on page 63.

FREEKEH. Also becoming trendy in the United States, freekeh is wheat that has been harvested while green and then lightly toasted so it has a slightly smoky flavor. While it's always been popular in North Africa, I've seen it recently at farmers' markets around New York City. As it cooks, it smells just like Genmai Cha tea, the Japanese green tea blended with toasted rice. Try with Marinated Tomatoes with Za'atar (page 145).

MILLET. This tiny gluten-free grain is a modern-day staple in Africa, India, and parts of China, as it grows well in drought-prone areas. Millet can cook up fluffy like couscous (which is best for salads) or be porridgy, like polenta. For a salad, try sprinkling it over Coconut-Roasted Squash Wedges with Lemongrass-Shallot Relish (page 157).

QUINOA. Because quinoa is one of the rare plant-based foods that provide all essential amino acids, this South American seed seems to have become the food of the century. Use it as the base of a salad or pop it in a dry skillet to use as a garnish. Try it with grilled zucchini and Cilantro–Pumpkin Seed Pesto (page 225).

RYE BERRIES. Grown in harsh wet climates, rye berries have a subtle tangy flavor that pairs well with Scandinavian, Russian, and other cool-weather flavors. Try it with Vegetarian Borscht Salad (page 166).

rye berries

millet

KAMUT AND CAULIFLOWER SALAD
WITH SMOKED ALMONDS AND MARMALADE DRESSING

VEGAN / SERVES 8 TO 16

1½ CUPS KAMUT, SPELT, OR OTHER WHEAT BERRY

4½ CUPS WATER

KOSHER SALT AND FRESHLY GROUND BLACK PEPPER

2 MEDIUM HEADS OF CAULIFLOWER (ABOUT 1¾ POUNDS EACH), CUT INTO BITE-SIZE FLORETS

½ CUP PLUS 2 TABLESPOONS EXTRA-VIRGIN OLIVE OIL

2 TABLESPOONS MINCED SHALLOT

¼ CUP SHERRY VINEGAR

2 TABLESPOONS ORANGE MARMALADE

1 CUP SMOKED OR TAMARI ALMONDS (ABOUT 6 OUNCES), CHOPPED, PLUS MORE FOR GARNISH

1 CUP BABY ARUGULA LEAVES, PLUS MORE FOR GARNISH

A cocktail I once had made with dry sherry and orange marmalade inspired the dressing for this sturdy cool-weather salad, which holds up beautifully at room temperature. The deep flavor of caramelized cauliflower and the smoked almonds make you question whether this salad really is vegan. (It is!)

While assisting cookbook author Lorna Sass with her book about whole grains many years ago, I learned about Kamut, a golden variety of wheat berry that has a lovely buttery flavor and a bouncy chew. If you can't find it, use any type of chewy grain. And if creating a vegan salad isn't a priority for you, a cup of crumbled salty feta cheese is a great addition.

NOTE. Grain salads seem to drink up salt, so check the seasoning before serving.

Preheat the oven to 400°F. Line 2 baking sheets with parchment paper.

In a large, heavy pot, combine the Kamut with the water and bring to a boil. Cover and simmer until tender, 45 to 60 minutes. Drain off any excess water and season with salt.

Spread the cauliflower on the baking sheets. Toss each with 2 tablespoons olive oil and add salt and pepper. Roast for 20 to 30 minutes, rotating the sheets halfway through, until the cauliflower is tender and browned in spots.

In a very large bowl, combine the shallot with the vinegar and let stand for 10 minutes. Whisk in the marmalade and then the remaining ¼ cup plus 2 tablespoons of olive oil. While still warm, add the Kamut and cauliflower and toss. Add the 1 cup almonds and 1 cup arugula and toss again. Season generously with salt and pepper.

Transfer the salad to a platter, garnish with arugula and almonds, and serve warm.

POTLUCK PREP. Without the arugula, the salad can be refrigerated overnight. Bring to room temperature and add the arugula and almonds within 1 hour of serving (see Note). The salad can stand at room temperature for 2 hours.

FREGOLA
WITH TUNA, CAPERS, AND SLOW-ROASTED TOMATOES

SERVES 6 TO 12

2 PINTS CHERRY TOMATOES, HALVED

4 GARLIC CLOVES, UNPEELED

3 TABLESPOONS EXTRA-VIRGIN OLIVE OIL

½ POUND FREGOLA PASTA

¼ CUP FRESH LEMON JUICE (FROM 2 TO 3 LEMONS)

2 (6- TO 7-OUNCE) CANS OR JARS TUNA PACKED IN OIL, DRAINED AND FLAKED

2 TABLESPOONS DRAINED CAPERS, ROUGHLY CHOPPED

1½ CUPS FRESH FLAT-LEAF PARSLEY LEAVES, ROUGHLY CHOPPED

KOSHER SALT AND FRESHLY GROUND BLACK PEPPER

½ CUP FRESH BASIL LEAVES, TORN

Oh, pasta salad. That ubiquitous picnic dish that foodies love to hate. Too often, it consists of gummy noodles saturated with bottled dressing and sprinkled with subpar vegetables. The day I was thinking about whether pasta salad could be modernized (or if it should be left to fade away, like Jell-O molds), I ordered lunch from my corner Italian restaurant. It was essentially a version of this salad—and it was absolutely delicious. When I set out to develop this recipe, I realized there is a recipe that's very similar on the bag of fregola I purchased. So, in the end, the recipe is not very modern at all—it's a classic dish from Sardinia, a lesser known part of Italy.

If you can't find bead-like fregola, you can substitute Israeli couscous, "frog-eye" pasta, or even pearled barley.

Preheat the oven to 225°F. Line a large rimmed baking sheet with parchment paper.

In a large bowl, toss the tomatoes and garlic with 1 tablespoon of the olive oil. Spread them out on the baking sheet, cut side up. Roast for about 3 hours (see Note), until they're mostly dried out with just a little moisture in the center. Let cool.

Bring a large pot of salted water to a boil, and cook the fregola according to the package directions until al dente. Drain well and rinse with cold water.

Squeeze the roasted garlic cloves out of their skins into a large bowl. Whisk in the lemon juice and the remaining 2 tablespoons olive oil. Add the warm fregola and tomatoes, along with the tuna, capers, and parsley and toss well. Season with salt and pepper and let stand for 10 minutes to let the flavors come together. Add the basil and season again with salt and pepper just before serving.

NOTE. Yep, true oven-dried tomatoes take that long. It's a good excuse to take a nap. If 3 hours has you panicked because you're due at your party in 45 minutes, you can also roast them at 400°F for 15 to 20 minutes. This higher heat will concentrate their flavors and lightly caramelize them. As a very last resort, you can toss them into the salad raw, but it won't be quite as succulent.

POTLUCK PREP. You can refrigerate this salad, without the basil, for up to 1 day. Serve it lightly chilled or at room temperature. Add the basil and re-season with salt and pepper just before serving.

SPICE-ROASTED CARROTS
WITH LENTILS

VEGAN (OPTIONAL); GLUTEN-FREE / SERVES 8 TO 16

FOR THE CARROTS

- 3 POUNDS REAL BABY CARROTS OR OTHER SMALL CARROTS, PREFERABLY MIXED COLORS, SCRUBBED IF ORGANIC, PEELED IF NOT
- 3 TABLESPOONS EXTRA-VIRGIN OLIVE OIL
- 1 TEASPOON GROUND CORIANDER
- 1 TEASPOON PAPRIKA
- 1 TEASPOON GROUND CUMIN
- KOSHER SALT AND FRESHLY GROUND BLACK PEPPER
- ½ CUP TENDER FRESH HERB LEAVES, SUCH AS CILANTRO, DILL, TARRAGON, MINT, AND/OR BASIL, ROUGHLY CHOPPED, PLUS MORE FOR GARNISH
- ¼ CUP FINELY SLICED PITTED MEDJOOL DATES, DRIED FIGS, OR PRUNES

FOR THE LENTILS

- 1 POUND DRIED BLACK BELUGA LENTILS OR FRENCH GREEN LENTILS
- KOSHER SALT AND FRESHLY GROUND BLACK PEPPER
- ¼ CUP EXTRA-VIRGIN OLIVE OIL
- 1 LARGE ONION, QUARTERED LENGTHWISE, PEELED, AND THINLY SLICED CROSSWISE
- 1 TABLESPOON MINCED GARLIC (ABOUT 2 LARGE CLOVES)
- 1 TEASPOON GROUND CORIANDER
- 1 TEASPOON GROUND CUMIN
- ½ TEASPOON GROUND CINNAMON
- 3 TABLESPOONS FRESH LEMON JUICE
- 1 CUP FRESH CILANTRO LEAVES, ROUGHLY CHOPPED
- PLAIN YOGURT, FOR SERVING (OPTIONAL)

At Vedge, one of my favorite restaurants in Philadelphia, chef Rich Landau makes carrot "schwarma" with black lentils, an incredible Middle Eastern–spiced dish that I constantly crave. It's flavorful and satisfying, as well as healthy without feeling overly virtuous. I end up making versions of his dish regularly from October to April. For this iteration, I add dates and tons of herbs. While this could certainly be a side dish for a large roast, I think it stands on its own as a vegetarian or vegan main course.

PREPARE THE CARROTS: Preheat the oven to 425°F. Line 2 large baking sheets with parchment paper.

In a large bowl, toss the carrots with the olive oil, coriander, paprika, and cumin, and season generously with salt and pepper. Spread the carrots out on the baking sheets.

Roast, rotating the baking sheets halfway through and shaking the carrots, for 20 to 30 minutes, until the carrots are nicely browned and tender. Let the carrots cool slightly, then transfer to a large bowl and toss with the herbs and dates.

MEANWHILE, PREPARE THE LENTILS: In a medium saucepan, cover the lentils with water by 2 inches and bring to a boil. Simmer over

(RECIPE CONTINUES)

medium heat until tender, 20 to 25 minutes. Drain the lentils, reserving ½ cup of the cooking liquid; season with salt.

In a deep skillet, heat the olive oil over medium heat. Add the onion and season generously with salt. Cook, stirring frequently until lightly browned, about 15 minutes. (If you want even more flavor, cook for 15 minutes longer for deeply browned onions.) Add the garlic, coriander, cumin, and cinnamon, and cook until fragrant, about 1 minute. Add the lentils and reserved cooking liquid, and cook until heated through, 2 to 3 minutes. Stir in the lemon juice and the cilantro.

Arrange the lentils on a platter and top with the carrots. Garnish with more herb leaves and dollops of yogurt on top (or alongside), if desired, and serve warm or at room temperature.

POTLUCK PREP. The lentils and roasted carrots, without the herbs and dates, can be refrigerated separately, overnight; bring to room temperature before serving. Bring the dish to the potluck already assembled with the vegetables on top of the lentils, then garnish with yogurt and extra herbs just before serving.

NO-BAKE SWEET PEA ENCHILADAS
WITH SOFRITO AND SEEDS

VEGETARIAN; GLUTEN-FREE / MAKES 12 ENCHILADAS

FOR THE SOFRITO

1 POUND CARROTS, COARSELY CHOPPED

1 SMALL YELLOW ONION, CHOPPED

5 GARLIC CLOVES

½ POUND RIPE TOMATOES, CHOPPED

½ CUP EXTRA-VIRGIN OLIVE OIL

1 TEASPOON CUMIN SEEDS

KOSHER SALT

1 TABLESPOON FRESH LIME JUICE

FOR THE FILLING

9 OUNCES QUESO BLANCO, COTIJA CHEESE, QUESO FRESCO, OR OTHER SALTY MILD CHEESE, CRUMBLED OR GRATED (ABOUT 2½ CUPS)

1½ CUPS FROZEN PEAS, THAWED

1½ CUPS FRESH CILANTRO LEAVES, ROUGHLY CHOPPED

¼ CUP FINELY CHOPPED WHITE ONION

FOR SERVING

GRAPESEED OIL, OR OTHER NEUTRAL OIL, FOR FRYING

16 (6- TO 7-INCH) CORN TORTILLAS

2 TABLESPOONS PUMPKIN SEEDS, LIGHTLY TOASTED

2 TABLESPOONS SUNFLOWER SEEDS, LIGHTLY TOASTED

1 HASS AVOCADO, CUT INTO SMALL CHUNKS AND TOSSED WITH LIME JUICE (OPTIONAL)

½ CUP FRESH TOMATILLO SALSA RECIPE (PAGE 225) OR STORE-BOUGHT MEXICAN SALSA VERDE (OPTIONAL)

This recipe has two different sources of inspiration. The first is Los Angeles chef Josef Centeno, who shared his great-grandmother's style of room temperature enchiladas with me for a story I edited at *Food & Wine*. As he does, I top my pea-filled tortillas with a carrot sofrito. But then, I take it a step further, garnishing the enchiladas with toasted seeds and avocado as an homage to the legendary carrot-avocado salad at New York City's ABC Kitchen.

MAKE THE SOFRITO: In a food processor, pulse the carrots, onion, and garlic until very finely chopped. Scrape the mixture into a medium bowl. Add the tomatoes to the food processor and pulse until nearly smooth.

In a deep, medium skillet, heat 2 tablespoons of the olive oil over medium heat until shimmering. Add the cumin seeds and toast until they pop, 1 to 2 minutes. Add the carrot mixture and a generous pinch of salt and cook, stirring every once in a while, until softened slightly and nearly dry, about 5 minutes. Add the tomato puree and cook, stirring occasionally, until most of the liquid has evaporated, 5 minutes. Stir in the remaining 6 tablespoons olive oil, reduce the heat to low, and cook, stirring occasionally,

(RECIPE CONTINUES)

until the carrots are very soft, about 1 hour and 30 minutes. Stir in the lime juice and season with salt. (Alternatively, you can bake the sofrito at 225°F, although calling them no-bake enchiladas is no longer quite true!)

MAKE THE FILLING: In a large bowl, toss the cheese with the peas, cilantro, and onion.

ASSEMBLE THE ENCHILADAS: In a small skillet, heat ¼ inch of the grapeseed oil. When the oil is warm, use tongs to cook the tortillas, one by one, until pliable, about 20 seconds for each. Transfer to a plate.

When the tortillas are cool enough to handle, place a scant ¼ cup of the pea-cheese filling onto each tortilla and roll up. Arrange them on a platter or shallow baking dish. (You may need to use more than one dish.) Spoon the sofrito on top, and sprinkle with the remaining filling, the pumpkin and sunflower seeds, and the avocado, if using. Serve with salsa, if desired.

POTLUCK PREP. The carrot sofrito, without the lime juice, can be refrigerated for up to 1 week; stir in the lime juice before using. The assembled enchiladas can stand at room temperature for about 2 hours.

VIETNAMESE-INSPIRED FISH ESCABECHE

GLUTEN-FREE / SERVES 8 TO 16

FOR THE BRINE

3 CUPS WATER

2 CUPS RICE VINEGAR

½ CUP SUGAR

2 TABLESPOONS PLUS
2 TEASPOONS KOSHER
SALT

1 MEDIUM CARROT,
VERY THINLY SLICED
INTO ROUNDS ON THE
DIAGONAL (ABOUT ¾ CUP)

½ SMALL DAIKON RADISH,
VERY THINLY SLICED
CROSSWISE ON THE
DIAGONAL (ABOUT ¾ CUP)

½ MEDIUM RED ONION,
HALVED AND THINLY
SLICED

1 TABLESPOON PEELED AND
JULIENNED FRESH GINGER
(FROM ABOUT 1-INCH
PIECE)

FOR THE FISH

2 POUNDS MILD WHITE FISH,
PREFERABLY WITHOUT
SKIN, SUCH AS FLOUNDER,
FLUKE, OCEAN PERCH,
SOLE, OR TROUT

1 CUP RICE FLOUR

2 TEASPOONS TURMERIC

GRAPESEED OIL OR OTHER
NEUTRAL OIL, FOR FRYING

KOSHER SALT

CHOPPED FRESH CILANTRO
AND DILL, FOR SERVING

Pickled fish is not the first thing most people associate with an American potluck, but maybe this gorgeous, vibrantly flavored dish will change their minds. In this version, which is based on a recipe by chef Paul Berglund of The Bachelor Farmer, in Minneapolis, the fish is fried first and then brined overnight (a preparation known as escabeche). The flavors are loosely inspired by an unusual but famous dish from Hanoi, in northern Vietnam, called *cha ca la Vong*, in which the fish is cooked in a turmeric-stained broth and garnished with dill along with other herbs.

You can serve the fish on plates with forks or with leaves of butter lettuce or iceberg, so people can wrap the fish in the leaves and eat it with their hands. Fried shallots (ones you make or even the premade kind you can find at Asian markets) or chopped roasted peanuts are great garnishes. Steamed white or brown rice is also a welcome addition to round this out into a larger meal.

POTLUCK PREP. The fish can be pickled up to 2 days ahead. You can drain the fish and vegetables, and arrange them on a platter or serve them straight from the marinade; either way, bring small containers of garnishes to add just before serving. The dish can stand at room temperature for up to 90 minutes, so it might be best to bring it in a cooler.

MAKE THE BRINE: In a nonreactive saucepan, combine the water with the vinegar, sugar, salt, carrot, radish, onion, and ginger, and bring to a boil. Simmer over medium-low heat, stirring occasionally, until the vegetables are slightly softened, about 10 minutes. Let cool.

MEANWHILE, PREPARE THE FISH: Cut the fish into pieces that are about 2 by 3 inches. You should have at least 10 pieces.

In a shallow bowl, whisk the rice flour with the turmeric.

In a very large nonstick or well-seasoned cast-iron skillet, add enough oil to lightly coat the bottom of the pan and heat it over medium-high heat. Season the fish lightly with salt and dredge in the flour mixture, dusting off the excess. Put the pieces of fish into the pan in a single layer without touching and cook until deep golden, 2½ minutes. Flip the fillets and fry until cooked through, about 2½ more minutes. Transfer the fish to a plate. Repeat with the remaining fish pieces, adding more oil as necessary.

Ladle half the brine and the vegetables into a large nonreactive baking dish or 2 smaller ones. Add the fish pieces and pour the remaining brine and vegetables on top. Cover the dish and refrigerate for 8 to 48 hours.

Garnish the fish with the cilantro and dill before serving.

OVEN-POACHED JAPANESE-INSPIRED SALMON
WITH TWO SAUCES

GLUTEN-FREE (OPTIONAL) / SERVES 8 TO 16

2 TABLESPOONS GRAPESEED OIL

1 POUND WHITE BUTTON MUSHROOMS, QUARTERED

1 MEDIUM ONION, CUT INTO ½-INCH WEDGES

12 CUPS WATER

1 (2-OUNCE) PACKAGE KOMBU

KOSHER SALT

1 (3-POUND) WILD OR SUSTAINABLY FARMED SALMON FILLET (GET IT WITHOUT SKIN IF YOU CAN)

FLAKY SALT, FOR SPRINKLING

SCALLION-GINGER RELISH, FOR SERVING (RECIPE FOLLOWS)

LEMON-SOY MAYONNAISE, FOR SERVING (RECIPE FOLLOWS)

This recipe is yet another mash-up of components from two great New York City chefs. The punchy and pungent relish is inspired by the beloved one from David Chang of the Momofuku empire. The broth, which I use to cook the salmon, comes from Ignacio Mattos of the wonderful sliver of a restaurant called Estela. A take on Japanese dashi, this broth adds a deep flavor to the fish and can be served afterward with noodles and a little of the scallion relish. If you're in a rush, however, you can simply poach the fish in 12 cups of salted water and serve with the sauces.

Preheat the oven to 300°F.

In a medium pot, heat the oil over medium-high heat. Add the mushrooms and onion and cook, stirring frequently, until nicely browned, 8 to 10 minutes. Add the water and bring to a boil. Reduce the heat to medium and simmer for 5 minutes. Remove the broth from the heat and add the kombu. Let stand for 10 to 15 minutes, until the broth is infused with the kombu flavor. Discard the kombu and season the broth generously with salt. Return the broth to a simmer.

Arrange the fish in a deep baking or roasting pan that's large enough to hold both fish and broth. Strain enough of the hot broth over the fish so it's submerged, discarding any onions and mushrooms. Cover the pan tightly with foil and bake the fish for 20 to 30 minutes, until slightly firm and a knife inserted in the center feels warm to the touch. Let the fish stand uncovered in the broth for 5 minutes.

Using 2 spatulas, transfer the fish to a platter or a clean baking dish; try to leave any skin behind. Use paper towels to dab off any white bits, and then spoon a few tablespoons of broth over the fish. Let the fish cool to room temperature, and then refrigerate until chilled, at least 1 hour. You can discard the broth or strain it to use for soup.

Just before serving, sprinkle the chilled fish with flaky salt and serve it with the relish and mayonnaise.

POTLUCK PREP. The poached fish and the accompanying sauces can be covered and refrigerated separately overnight. The chilled fish can stand at room temperature for only about 90 minutes, so transport it in a cooler, if necessary.

LEMON-SOY MAYONNAISE

MAKES ABOUT 1 CUP

1 CUP MAYONNAISE

1 TABLESPOON LOW-SODIUM SOY SAUCE (USE GLUTEN-FREE, IF NECESSARY)

1 TABLESPOON FRESH LEMON JUICE

In a small bowl, blend together the mayonnaise, soy sauce, and lemon juice.

SCALLION-GINGER RELISH

MAKES ABOUT 2 CUPS

12 THINLY SLICED SCALLIONS (2½ CUPS)

½ CUP FINELY MINCED PEELED FRESH GINGER (FROM A FAT 3-INCH PIECE)

½ CUP GRAPESEED OR OTHER NEUTRAL OIL

2 TEASPOONS LOW-SODIUM SOY SAUCE (USE GLUTEN-FREE IF NECESSARY)

1 TEASPOON FRESH LEMON JUICE

KOSHER SALT

In a medium bowl, combine the scallions, ginger, oil, soy sauce, and lemon juice. Season with salt and let stand for 15 minutes, until the scallions are wilted.

VARIATION. Stir-fry the scallions and ginger in 1 tablespoon of oil for 1 to 2 minutes, until they lose their bite. Let cool, and then mix with the remaining ingredients.

CHINESE CHICKEN SALAD
WITH SESAME-GINGER DRESSING

GLUTEN-FREE (OPTIONAL) / SERVES 8 TO 16

FOR THE DRESSING

¼ CUP FRESH LEMON JUICE

3 TABLESPOONS LOW-SODIUM SOY SAUCE (USE GLUTEN-FREE IF NECESSARY)

2 TABLESPOONS HONEY

2 TABLESPOONS RICE VINEGAR

2 TEASPOONS TAHINI

1 (1½-INCH) PIECE PEELED FRESH GINGER, FINELY GRATED

½ TO 1 TEASPOON CHILI-GARLIC SAUCE, PLUS MORE TO TASTE (USE GLUTEN-FREE IF NECESSARY)

½ CUP GRAPESEED OIL OR OTHER NEUTRAL OIL

FOR THE SALAD

1 LARGE NAPA CABBAGE (ABOUT 2½ POUNDS), OUTER LEAVES REMOVED, HEAD HALVED, AND LEAVES SHREDDED CROSSWISE

1 (3-POUND) ROTISSERIE CHICKEN, CHILLED OR AT ROOM TEMPERATURE, MEAT PULLED OFF THE BONES INTO BITE-SIZE PIECES (ABOUT 3 CUPS)

2 CUPS SHREDDED CARROTS, OR 4 MEDIUM CARROTS, JULIENNED

6 OUNCES SUGAR SNAP PEAS OR SNOW PEAS, THINLY SLICED CROSSWISE ON THE DIAGONAL

1 CUP FRESH CILANTRO LEAVES, ROUGHLY CHOPPED, PLUS MORE FOR GARNISH

¾ CUP SALT-AND-PEPPER CANDIED CASHEWS (PAGE 220) OR ROASTED SALTED CASHEWS, ROUGHLY CHOPPED

This sweet-and-crunchy style of chicken salad is probably more retro Californian than "Chinese." For a more modern take, I have skipped the canned mandarin oranges and fried wontons and substituted napa cabbage for the usual lettuce. If you can find other Asian greens, like tatsoi, mizuna, and mustard greens, and you're not worried about their wilting, definitely add them to the mix.

MAKE THE DRESSING: In a medium bowl, whisk the lemon juice with the soy sauce, honey, rice vinegar, tahini, ginger, and ½ teaspoon chili-garlic sauce. Gradually add the oil, whisking constantly.

Taste the dressing and add another ½ teaspoon chili-garlic sauce if you'd like it spicier.

ASSEMBLE THE SALAD: In a large bowl, toss the cabbage with the chicken, carrots, peas, and 1 cup cilantro leaves.

Within 15 minutes of serving, drizzle the salad with three-fourths of the dressing, add the cashews, and toss. Add the remaining dressing, if desired, then garnish with additional cilantro, and serve with more chili-garlic sauce on the side.

POTLUCK PREP. While the salad stays crunchy, it does tend to release a lot of water. For that reason, it's best to dress it within a few minutes of serving it. If you're traveling with the salad, put the dressing in a jar (which makes it easy to shake if it separates) and keep the cashews in a separate container. Then just bring it all together soon before serving.

CORNMEAL-CRUSTED OVEN-FRIED CHICKEN
TO SERVE COLD

GLUTEN-FREE (OPTIONAL) / MAKES 20 PIECES OF CHICKEN

FOR THE BRINE

1 CUP KOSHER SALT

½ CUP SUGAR

1 CUP WATER

1 HEAD FRESH GARLIC, TOP REMOVED AND HEAD SMASHED

1 TABLESPOON CORIANDER SEEDS

6 BAY LEAVES

1 TEASPOON WHOLE BLACK PEPPERCORNS

15 CUPS ICE WATER

10 SMALL TO MEDIUM CHICKEN DRUMSTICKS

10 SMALL TO MEDIUM CHICKEN THIGHS

FOR THE COATING

2 CUPS BUTTERMILK

2 CUPS ALL-PURPOSE FLOUR OR RICE FLOUR (FOR GLUTEN-FREE)

¾ CUP FINE CORNMEAL

1½ TEASPOONS KOSHER SALT

1 TEASPOON GROUND CORIANDER

1 TEASPOON CAYENNE PEPPER

1 TEASPOON FRESHLY GROUND BLACK PEPPER

OIL OR NONSTICK COOKING SPRAY

Cold fried chicken is the ultimate picnic food, even if it inspires some hatred (there are people who believe that fried chicken *must* be served hot and only hot). After a bit of experimentation, I realized that oven-fried chicken is nearly as good as the real stuff when it's cold because, either way, it loses that shattering crisp coating. Since oven-frying is healthier, less labor intensive, and less messy, it's a winning technique for potluck.

If you wish, you can certainly use this brine and coating to make real fried chicken. Because the cornmeal burns quickly if it gets too hot, it's better to deep-fry than to shallow-fry.

BRINE THE CHICKEN: In a medium pot, combine the salt and sugar with the water and cook over medium heat, stirring constantly, until the salt and sugar dissolve. Transfer to a large bowl, add the garlic, coriander, bay leaves, peppercorns, and ice water, and stir until the brine is cold. Add the chicken, cover, and refrigerate for 8 to 24 hours.

COAT AND COOK THE CHICKEN: Remove the chicken from the brine and let stand for 30 minutes to take off some of the chill. Flick off any spices that remain on the chicken.

Preheat the oven to 450°F. Line 2 large rimmed baking sheets with foil (for easier clean-up) and rub with a thin coating of oil or spray with nonstick cooking spray.

Put the buttermilk in a shallow bowl. In another shallow bowl, whisk the flour with the cornmeal, salt, coriander, cayenne, and pepper.

Working in batches, dip the chicken in the buttermilk and then dredge in the flour mixture, shaking off the excess. Transfer the chicken pieces to the prepared baking sheet, skin side down for the thighs.

Roast the chicken, rotating the pans halfway through, for 25 to 30 minutes, until very browned. Flip the chicken pieces and roast for 5 to 10 minutes longer, until browned and an instant-read thermometer inserted into the thickest parts registers about 165°F. Transfer the chicken to a wire rack and let cool for at least 10 minutes. Serve hot, room temperature, or cold.

POTLUCK PREP. If you are the host or you're not going far for a party, you can absolutely serve the chicken warm. Just pack it in a single layer in containers that you don't have to cover, thereby preventing it from steaming. To serve it cold, let it cool completely at room temperature—this will take at least 1 hour— then refrigerate for at least 2 hours so it's nice and cold. The chicken will stay good in the refrigerator for up to 2 days.

DANIEL'S TACOS DE CANASTA

GLUTEN-FREE / MAKES ABOUT 40 TACOS

40 BEST-QUALITY SOFT CORN TORTILLAS, PLUS A FEW EXTRA IN CASE OF TEARING

GUAJILLO SAUCE (RECIPE FOLLOWS), KEPT HOT

POTATO-CHORIZO FILLING (RECIPE FOLLOWS), WARMED

1 LARGE WHITE ONION, THINLY SLICED

REFRIED BEANS (RECIPE FOLLOWS), WARMED

AVOCADO SALSA VERDE (RECIPE FOLLOWS), FOR SERVING

"Nobody thinks that tacos can be potluck food," my friend and former coworker, Daniel Gritzer, told me. After a trip to Mexico City, he discovered otherwise. "Tacos de canasta," he said, are the answer. "Basically they are pre-made corn tacos that are packed into a paper-lined basket. The tortillas get kind of moist and a little oily, but in a good way, and you just unpack the tacos as people eat their way through them."

If you spend any time with Daniel, you learn quickly his idea of a simple dish doesn't jive with the average home cook's idea of simple. Still, this dish is worth making for a large party because people won't stop talking about it. It has a lot of components, but only three are nonnegotiable: the onion, the tortillas, and the Guajillo Sauce. Otherwise, you can vary the fillings (just make sure they are on the dry side) or substitute pre-made refried beans or jarred salsa—just don't tell Daniel. (See photograph on pages 56–57.)

Preheat the oven to 225°F.

Divide the tortillas into stacks of 10 and wrap each stack in aluminum foil. Transfer to the oven and allow them to warm, at least 30 minutes.

Heat a large enameled cast-iron Dutch oven (about 5-quart capacity) over medium heat until warm; remove from heat. Drizzle warmed Guajillo Sauce all over the Dutch oven, brushing with a pastry brush to distribute evenly, and scatter with a layer of the onion.

Remove 1 packet of warmed tortillas from the oven and tear open. Working with 1 tortilla at a time and wearing a clean glove if necessary to protect your hand from the heat, spread a small amount of potato filling on half the tortilla, then fold the tortilla in half over the filling to close, forming a half-moon shape. Set in the bottom of the Dutch oven. Continue filling tortillas with potato filling and arranging in an even layer in bottom of the Dutch oven until the first layer is complete. Scatter a small amount of sliced onion on top and generously brush Guajillo Sauce all over with a pastry brush.

Make another layer of tacos, filling these with the refried beans. Continue layering potato and refried-bean tacos, removing foil packets of tortillas from the oven as needed, and scattering each layer with onion and brushing with hot Guajillo Sauce, until the Dutch oven is full or you have no remaining tortillas. (Reserve any remaining potato filling and refried beans for another use.) Cover the Dutch oven and transfer it to the oven.

Bake for about 45 minutes, until the tacos are warmed through. Then let stand at room temperature for up to 1 hour. (This can be your travel time.)

To serve, use a spatula to carefully lift each taco out of the Dutch oven along with some of the onion, and spoon salsa verde generously on top.

POTLUCK PREP. You can wrap the warmed Dutch oven in a thick towel or blanket to transport it to your party. Alternatively, you can assemble the tacos and warm them at the host's house.

GUAJILLO SAUCE

MAKES ABOUT 2½ CUPS

    6 GUAJILLO CHILES, STEMMED, SEEDED, AND
      TORN INTO PIECES

    3 GARLIC CLOVES

    2 CUPS THINLY SLICED WHITE ONION
      (ABOUT 1 WHITE ONION)

    2 CUPS SAFFLOWER OIL

    KOSHER SALT

Heat a large cast-iron skillet over high heat until nearly smoking. Add the chiles, garlic, and onion and cook, turning occasionally, until charred in spots, about 4 minutes. Reduce the heat to medium, add 1 cup of the oil, and fry, stirring occasionally, until the onion and chiles are just tender, about 3 minutes. Let cool to warm.

Scrape the vegetables and oil into a blender. Add the remaining 1 cup oil and a large pinch of salt. Cover and blend, starting at low speed and gradually increasing to high speed, until a smooth puree forms. Season with salt and keep warm. (The sauce can be refrigerated for up to 3 days; reheat gently before using.)

POTATO-CHORIZO FILLING

MAKES ABOUT 8 CUPS

    3 POUNDS RUSSET POTATOES (ABOUT
      6 LARGE), PEELED, CUT INTO 1-INCH
      PIECES, AND RINSED UNDER COLD WATER

    KOSHER SALT AND FRESHLY GROUND
      BLACK PEPPER

    1¾ POUNDS MEXICAN FRESH CHORIZO,
      CASINGS REMOVED

    4 TABLESPOONS UNSALTED BUTTER

In a medium pot, cover the potatoes with water and season generously with salt. Bring to a simmer over medium-high heat and cook until the potatoes can be pierced easily with a fork, about 15 minutes. Drain and set aside.

In a large skillet, cook the chorizo over medium-high heat, stirring frequently and using a potato masher or spoon to break the chorizo into small pieces, until the fat has rendered and the chorizo is cooked through, about 8 minutes. Reduce the heat to medium and add the potatoes. Using a potato masher, mash the potatoes thoroughly. Stir in the butter and season with salt and pepper. Keep warm. (The filling can be made up to a day in advance and refrigerated in an airtight container; reheat before using.)

(RECIPE CONTINUES)

REFRIED BEANS

MAKES ABOUT 7 CUPS

½ CUP LARD OR VEGETABLE OIL

1 MEDIUM WHITE ONION, MINCED
(ABOUT 1 CUP)

6½ CUPS COOKED PINTO BEANS (FROM ABOUT
1 POUND DRIED OR FOUR 15-OUNCE CANS)

2 CUPS BEAN COOKING LIQUID OR WATER,
PLUS MORE AS NEEDED

KOSHER SALT

In a large skillet, heat the lard or oil over medium-high heat until shimmering. Add the onion and cook, stirring occasionally, until softened and lightly browned, about 7 minutes. Stir in the beans and bean cooking liquid. Using a potato masher or the back of a wooden spoon, smash the beans to form a chunky paste. Reduce the heat to medium and cook, stirring, until desired consistency is reached. If the refried beans are too dry, add more bean cooking liquid, 1 tablespoon at a time, as needed. Season with salt and keep warm. (The refried beans can be made up to 3 days in advance and refrigerated in an airtight container; reheat before using.)

AVOCADO SALSA VERDE

MAKES ABOUT 5 CUPS

1½ POUNDS TOMATILLOS, HUSKS AND STEMS
REMOVED

1 MEDIUM WHITE ONION (12 OUNCES),
QUARTERED

2 JALAPEÑOS OR SERRANO CHILES,
STEMMED, HALVED, AND SEEDED

4 GARLIC CLOVES

1 LOOSELY PACKED CUP FRESH CILANTRO
LEAVES AND TENDER STEMS

1 MEDIUM HASS AVOCADO, HALVED, PITTED,
AND SCOOPED

¼ CUP FRESH LIME JUICE (ABOUT 2 LIMES)

KOSHER SALT

In a medium pot, cover the tomatillos, onion, and chiles with water and bring to a boil over high heat. Lower the heat to medium and simmer, turning the tomatillos occasionally, until the vegetables are tender, about 10 minutes. Drain.

Transfer the vegetables to a blender and add the garlic, cilantro, avocado, and lime juice. Blend until smooth. Season with salt. Refrigerate until ready to use. (The salsa can be refrigerated in an airtight container overnight.)

SPICED BUTTERFLIED LAMB
WITH DATE BARBECUE SAUCE

GLUTEN-FREE / SERVES 12 TO 20

1 TABLESPOON PLUS
1½ TEASPOONS
CORIANDER SEEDS

1 TABLESPOON CUMIN SEEDS

1 TABLESPOON CARAWAY
SEEDS

1 TABLESPOON FENNEL
SEEDS

1 TABLESPOON PAPRIKA

1½ TEASPOONS GROUND
CINNAMON

KOSHER SALT AND
FRESHLY GROUND
BLACK PEPPER

½ CUP EXTRA-VIRGIN
OLIVE OIL

1 (7-POUND) BUTTERFLIED
LEG OF LAMB, TRIMMED
OF EXCESS FAT

10 GARLIC CLOVES, 4 THINLY
SLICED AND 6 MINCED

1 LARGE ONION, FINELY
CHOPPED

¼ CUP PLUS 2 TABLESPOONS
TOMATO PASTE

1 QUART LOW-SODIUM,
CLUTEN-FREE BEEF BROTH

3 TABLESPOONS HONEY

¼ TEASPOON SAFFRON,
CRUMBLED INTO
1 TABLESPOON WATER

½ TEASPOON CAYENNE
PEPPER

12 PITTED LARGE MEDJOOL
DATES, MINCED (ABOUT
½ CUP)

¼ CUP FRESH LEMON JUICE,
PLUS MORE TO TASTE

½ POUND LARGE GREEN
OLIVES, FINELY CHOPPED
(ABOUT 1¼ CUPS)

½ CUP FINELY CHOPPED
FRESH MINT

½ CUP FINELY CHOPPED
FRESH CILANTRO

Butterflied leg of lamb is one of the best cuts of meat to serve when throwing an impromptu party. Just rub it with some olive oil, garlic, and salt, and grill it over medium-high heat (or you can broil it). It's so thin that it won't take more than 15 minutes per side. If you leave the thickest parts rare to medium-rare, the thinner parts will be cooked a bit more, giving you meat for every preference. After you take the lamb off the heat, just let it rest for 5 minutes before you thinly slice it across the grain. You can eat it hot or at room temperature and even cold; and it's great alongside all kinds of salads.

For a leg of lamb that's a little more impressive and boldly flavored, try this recipe. I've taken cues from Moroccan spices and flavors to make a rub for the meat and a sticky date-sweetened sauce.

(RECIPE CONTINUES)

In a small skillet, toast the coriander and the cumin, caraway, and fennel seeds until fragrant, 1 to 2 minutes. Let cool, and then finely grind the seeds to a powder in a spice grinder. Transfer to a small bowl. Add the paprika, cinnamon, and 1 teaspoon pepper. Set aside 3 tablespoons of the spice mixture for the sauce, then stir 1½ teaspoons of salt and ¼ cup of the olive oil into the remaining spice mixture.

Using a small, sharp knife, make ½-inch-deep slits all over the lamb. Press the garlic slices into the slits. Coat the lamb with the spiced oil, making sure to rub it into the slits. Cover with plastic wrap and refrigerate for at least 6 hours or for up to 24 hours.

Meanwhile, in a medium saucepan, heat the remaining ¼ cup olive oil over medium-low heat. Add the onion and minced garlic and cook, stirring occasionally, until softened, about 10 minutes. Add the reserved 3 tablespoons of the spice mixture and cook, stirring occasionally, until fragrant, about 4 minutes. Add the tomato paste and cook, stirring, for 1 minute. Add the beef broth, honey, saffron water, and cayenne, then increase the heat to high and cook until the sauce is slightly thickened, about 8 minutes. Add the minced dates, reduce the heat to low, and simmer, stirring occasionally, until they break down and the sauce is thick and glossy, about 15 minutes. Remove from the heat. Stir in the lemon juice and season the sauce with salt, pepper, and more lemon juice. Reserve ½ cup of the date barbecue sauce for glazing the lamb.

Light a grill or preheat the broiler and arrange the rack about 4 inches from the heat. Lightly season the lamb with salt and pepper. Grill over moderate heat, turning once, until the lamb is nicely charred all over and an instant-read thermometer inserted in the thickest part of the leg registers 125°F for medium-rare, about 15 minutes per side. During the last 3 minutes of grilling, brush the ½ cup date barbecue sauce all over the lamb. Transfer the grilled lamb to a carving board and let rest for 5 to 10 minutes.

In a small bowl, toss the olives with the mint and cilantro. Slice the lamb across the grain and serve with the remaining date barbecue sauce and the olive relish.

POTLUCK PREP. The date barbecue sauce can be kept in an airtight container and refrigerated for up to 3 days. If you're not hosting, either ask to use the host's grill or grill the meat at home without the sauce. After the lamb cools, cut it crosswise into large chunks that can be easily wrapped in plastic and refrigerate for a few hours or overnight. When you get to the potluck, slice the meat just before serving, putting the sauce and relish on the side.

ROSEMARY-GARLIC–BRINED PORK LOIN
WITH PISTACHIO SALSA VERDE

GLUTEN-FREE / SERVES 8 TO 16

FOR THE BRINE AND PORK

4 CUPS WATER

¾ CUP KOSHER SALT

½ CUP SUGAR

1 HEAD OF GARLIC, HALVED HORIZONTALLY

ZEST OF 1 LEMON, REMOVED IN STRIPS WITH A VEGETABLE PEELER

3 FRESH ROSEMARY SPRIGS

2 BAY LEAVES

1 TEASPOON BLACK PEPPERCORNS

8 CUPS ICE WATER

1 (3½-POUND) CENTER-CUT PORK LOIN ROAST

FOR THE RUB

4 GARLIC CLOVES, SMASHED

KOSHER SALT

2 TABLESPOONS ROUGHLY CHOPPED FRESH ROSEMARY LEAVES

¼ CUP EXTRA-VIRGIN OLIVE OIL

2 TABLESPOONS GRAPESEED OR OTHER NEUTRAL OIL

PISTACHIO SALSA VERDE (PAGE 226), FOR SERVING (OPTIONAL)

Even well-marbled pork loin from sustainably raised pigs is relatively lean, so brining it is a great way to go. The method not only seasons throughout but also keeps it extra juicy. Because the pork is brined for at least a half day, it essentially cures, making it perfect for serving at room temperature or even chilled.

The salty-tangy salsa verde is great alongside, or you can keep it simple, slicing the meat thin for sandwiches and serving it with mayonnaise or your favorite mustard.

POTLUCK PREP. The cooked pork loin can be refrigerated for up to 3 days. It can stand at room temperature for up to 2 hours. Slice it right at the table or within 1 hour of serving.

BRINE THE PORK: In a medium saucepan, bring the water, salt, and sugar to a simmer over medium-high heat, stirring to dissolve. Pour into a very large heatproof bowl or baking pan. Add the garlic, lemon zest, rosemary, bay leaves, peppercorns, and ice water. Stir. When cold, add the pork, cover, and refrigerate for 12 to 24 hours.

RUB AND ROAST THE PORK: Remove the pork from the brine and pat dry. Let stand for 30 minutes. Preheat the oven to 350°F. Set a baking rack over a baking sheet or a roasting rack in a roasting pan.

In a mortar or on a cutting board, smash the garlic with a pinch of salt to form a paste. Mix the paste with the rosemary and the olive oil. Rub half the paste on the lean side of the pork roast.

In a very large skillet or a large griddle, heat the grapeseed oil. Add the pork fat side down and cook over medium-high heat until very browned, 4 to 5 minutes. Transfer the pork to the rack fat side up and rub with the remaining paste.

Roast the pork for 50 to 60 minutes, until the pork registers 140°F on an instant-read thermometer. Let rest for at least 10 minutes before slicing. Serve with the salsa verde, if desired.

FLANK STEAK LETTUCE CUPS
WITH LIME-HOISIN DRESSING

GLUTEN-FREE (OPTIONAL) / SERVES 8 TO 12

FOR THE STEAK

2 (1½- TO 1¾-POUND) FLANK STEAKS, PREFERABLY GRASS-FED, EACH CUT CROSSWISE INTO 3 PIECES

1 MEDIUM YELLOW ONION

4 GARLIC CLOVES, SMASHED

1 (2-INCH) PIECE FRESH GINGER, QUARTERED

1 STAR ANISE

3 WHOLE CLOVES

1 CINNAMON STICK

KOSHER SALT

FOR THE SALAD

2 TABLESPOONS FRESH LIME JUICE, PLUS LIME WEDGES FOR SERVING

4 TEASPOONS ASIAN FISH SAUCE

4 TEASPOONS HOISIN SAUCE (USE GLUTEN-FREE)

1 TEASPOON SRIRACHA, PLUS MORE FOR SERVING

KOSHER SALT

6 SCALLIONS, THINLY SLICED (½ CUP)

1 CUP FRESH CILANTRO, PLUS MORE FOR SERVING

1 CUP FRESH MINT LEAVES, PLUS MORE FOR SERVING

BUTTER LETTUCE LEAVES, FOR SERVING

Flank steak is typically grilled or seared and served medium-rare, but this recipe will convince you to try this lean and relatively affordable cut of beef another way: boiled (yep!). This recipe is a Vietnamese take on a Mexican dish known as *salpicón* of beef, in which the steak is simmered in an aromatic liquid. Here, the meat is shredded for a room-temperature salad. Plus, as a bonus, you get a resulting broth that you can use to boil noodles for a faux *pho*.

POTLUCK PREP. The shredded beef can be refrigerated overnight and served lightly chilled or at room temperature. Add the dressing and herbs within 1 hour of serving.

COOK THE STEAK: In a very large pot, combine the steak, onion, garlic, ginger, star anise, cloves, and cinnamon stick. Cover the steak with at least 2 inches of water. Bring to a boil, reduce the heat to medium-low, and simmer, skimming off any foam, until the beef pulls easily with a fork, about 40 minutes. Remove the pan from the heat and let cool to room temperature.

Transfer the steak to a large bowl and finely shred the meat, discarding any fat. Add ½ cup of the cooking liquid, season with salt, and let stand for 5 minutes. Strain the remaining cooking liquid and refrigerate for another use.

PREPARE THE SALAD: In a small bowl, whisk the lime juice with the fish sauce, hoisin sauce, and 1 teaspoon of Sriracha. Pour the dressing over the beef and toss. Season with salt and add the scallions, 1 cup cilantro, and 1 cup of the mint to the salad and gently toss.

Arrange the beef salad on a platter with tongs. Arrange the lettuce leaves and the additional herbs and lime wedges on another platter and serve with Sriracha on the side.

SLOW-COOKED & SERVED HOT

MASSAMAN-MUSHROOM CURRY

VEGAN (OPTIONAL) / SERVES 6 TO 8

- ¼ CUP PLUS 2 TABLESPOONS GRAPESEED OR OTHER NEUTRAL OIL
- 1 LARGE ONION, CHOPPED
- KOSHER SALT
- 2 LARGE YUKON GOLD POTATOES (ABOUT 1 POUND), CUT INTO ½-INCH PIECES
- 8 LARGE PORTOBELLO MUSHROOM CAPS, CUT INTO 1-INCH PIECES

- 1 (4-OUNCE) CAN MAESRI MASSAMAN CURRY PASTE (ABOUT ⅓ CUP)
- 2 (14-OUNCE) CANS COCONUT MILK
- 2 CUPS VEGETABLE BROTH
- 2 TABLESPOONS LOW-SODIUM SOY SAUCE OR FISH SAUCE
- 2 TABLESPOONS FRESH LIME JUICE, PLUS MORE TO TASTE

- STEAMED JASMINE RICE (OPTIONAL), FOR SERVING
- CHOPPED UNSALTED PEANUTS, FOR SERVING
- CHOPPED FRESH CILANTRO LEAVES, FOR SERVING
- LIME WEDGES, FOR SERVING

I really love the Maesri massaman curry paste here, because it's fragrant and lightly spicy. It's available at many supermarkets and from Amazon, but if you can't find it, you can make a different but still delicious curry with Thai red curry paste. Since red curry paste is spicier, start with half the amount and increase to your liking, adding more lime juice as desired. I keep this recipe very simple, with just the two vegetables, but you can absolutely add others. Cauliflower or winter squash, for example, would work well; you could also throw in some spinach right before serving.

POTLUCK PREP. The curry can be refrigerated overnight. Reheat gently on the stovetop or in a slow-cooker set to high.

In an enameled cast-iron Dutch oven or large, heavy pot, heat 2 tablespoons of the oil over medium-high heat. Add the onion, season with salt, and cook, stirring, until softened, about 5 minutes. Add the potatoes and cook, stirring constantly, until browned in spots, about 5 minutes. Scrape into a bowl.

In the same pot, heat the remaining ¼ cup oil over medium-high heat. Add the mushrooms, season with salt, cover, and cook until they start to release their liquid, about 4 minutes. Uncover the pot and cook until all the liquid has evaporated and the mushrooms are brown, about 15 minutes longer. Add the curry paste and cook until fragrant, about 2 minutes. Return the onion and potatoes to the pot, add the coconut milk and vegetable broth, and bring to a boil, scraping up any browned bits on the bottom of the pan. Simmer over medium heat until the potatoes are tender and the liquid is thick enough to coat the mushrooms, about 20 minutes.

Add the soy sauce and 2 tablespoons of the lime juice. Season with more salt and lime juice, as desired. Serve hot, over steamed rice and with the peanuts, cilantro, and lime wedges.

MISO-AND-MOLASSES BAKED BEANS

VEGAN / SERVES 8 TO 16

- 1 POUND HIGH-QUALITY DRIED NAVY OR CANNELLINI BEANS, SOAKED OVERNIGHT AND DRAINED
- 8 CUPS VEGETABLE STOCK OR WATER
- ¼ CUP PLUS 2 TABLESPOONS MOLASSES

- ¼ CUP PLUS 2 TABLESPOONS CIDER VINEGAR, PLUS MORE FOR SEASONING
- ¼ CUP PLUS 2 TABLESPOONS MISO, PREFERABLY RED BUT ANY MISO IS FINE
- 2 TABLESPOONS LOW-SODIUM SOY SAUCE
- 1½ TABLESPOONS DRY MUSTARD

- 1 LARGE GARLIC CLOVE, FINELY GRATED
- 1 TEASPOON SMOKED PAPRIKA (SUCH AS SPANISH PIMENTÓN DE LA VERA)
- 1½ TEASPOONS FINELY GRATED PEELED FRESH GINGER (FROM ABOUT A 3-INCH PIECE)
- KOSHER SALT

These baked beans are New England style in spirit. That's to say that I skip the tomato-based sauce in favor of one flavored with molasses. To give the beans a satisfying depth of flavor but still keep them vegan, I add miso, fresh ginger, and soy sauce. While I pulled these three ingredients from the Asian pantry, the beans, in the end, just taste like really good baked beans.

POTLUCK PREP. You can refrigerate the baked beans overnight and reheat them gently, adding a little water if you need to loosen them, before serving. You can also serve these from a slow cooker, if desired.

In an enameled cast-iron casserole or other heavy, ovenproof pot with a lid, cover the beans with the stock or water and bring to a boil. Reduce the heat to low and simmer, skimming off the foam, until the skins curl up when you blow on them, 20 to 30 minutes.

Preheat the oven to 350°F.

In a medium bowl, whisk the molasses with the vinegar, miso, soy sauce, mustard, garlic, paprika, and ginger. Add to the beans and return to a boil.

Cover and bake the beans, stirring every 30 minutes or so, for about 1½ hours, until the beans are very tender and the liquid thickens slightly. (The liquid will thicken even more as the beans sit.)

Season the beans with salt and more vinegar, if desired, and serve.

VARIATION. If you'd like some meat with your beans, add a sliced cured sausage, such as kielbasa, during the last 30 minutes of cooking.

HEIDI'S RIBOLLITA AND LEMON-CHILE RELISH

VEGAN / SERVES 10 OR MORE

FOR THE RIBOLLITA

- ¼ CUP EXTRA-VIRGIN OLIVE OIL, PLUS MORE FOR DRIZZLING
- 4 CELERY STALKS, CHOPPED
- 4 GARLIC CLOVES, CHOPPED
- 2 MEDIUM CARROTS, CHOPPED (OR 2 CUPS PEELED AND CHOPPED WINTER SQUASH)
- 1 MEDIUM ONION, CHOPPED
- FINE-GRAIN SEA SALT
- 1 (14-OUNCE) CAN WHOLE OR CRUSHED TOMATOES
- 1 POUND CAVOLO NERO (LACINATO KALE, OR TUSCAN KALE), STEMS TRIMMED AND LEAVES WELL CHOPPED
- 4 CUPS COOKED WHITE BEANS, SUCH AS CANNELLINI (OR THREE 15-OUNCE CANS, DRAINED)
- 8 CUPS WATER
- ½ POUND CRUSTLESS LOAF OF BREAD

FOR THE RELISH

- 2 LARGE ANCHO CHILES
- 6 TABLESPOONS EXTRA-VIRGIN OLIVE OIL
- 2 GARLIC CLOVES, SMASHED
- 1 WHOLE PRESERVED LEMON, FLESH SEEDED, PEEL AND FLESH MINCED
- ¼ TEASPOON FINE-GRAIN SEA SALT

Heidi Swanson of *101Cookbooks*, the online recipe journal, is a brilliant cook. When she launched her blog and began writing her cookbooks, she rarely mentioned that her recipes were vegetarian. She wanted them to be delicious in their own right. (And they are.) She has an incredible knack for taking something familiar, like this ribollita, and twisting it slightly so it seems fresh and modern. And like all great cooks, Heidi knows the importance of a good garnish. Here, she makes a spectacular relish of smoky ancho chiles and salty Moroccan preserved lemons to top this Mediterranean soup.

MAKE THE RIBOLLITA: In your largest thick-bottomed pot set over medium heat, combine the ¼ cup olive oil with the celery, garlic, carrots, onion, and 1½ teaspoons salt. Cook for 10 to 15 minutes, sweating the vegetables, but avoid any browning. Stir in the tomatoes, using the back of the spoon to break them up a bit, and simmer for about 10 more minutes, until thickened. Stir in the cavolo nero, 3 cups of the beans, and the water. Bring to a boil, reduce the heat to medium-low, and simmer until the greens are tender, about 10 minutes.

Meanwhile, mash or puree the remaining beans with a generous splash of water. Tear the bread into bite-size chunks. Stir the beans and bread into the soup. Simmer, stirring occasionally, until the bread breaks down and the soup thickens, 20 to 30 more minutes.

MAKE THE RELISH: Remove the stem, ribs, and seeds from the chiles. Using scissors, snip the chiles into very small, irregular pieces. In a small pot set over medium heat, combine the olive oil, garlic, and chile pieces. Cook, tilting the pan so that the oil pools, toasting the chiles, but take care not to burn the garlic, for about 5 minutes. Remove the pan from the heat. Use a potato masher or the bottom of an ice cream scoop to smash the garlic pieces. Stir in the preserved lemon and salt.

Season the soup with more salt, if desired. Serve the soup with the lemon-chile relish on the side.

POTLUCK PREP. The soup and relish can be refrigerated separately overnight. (In fact, the soup is better if served the next day.) Bring the relish to room temperature and reheat the soup gently. Serve from the stovetop or a slow cooker.

TOMATILLO PULLED CHICKEN

GLUTEN-FREE (OPTIONAL) / SERVES 8 TO 12

3 TABLESPOONS EXTRA-
VIRGIN OLIVE OIL

4 POUNDS BONELESS,
SKINLESS CHICKEN THIGHS

KOSHER SALT AND
FRESHLY GROUND
BLACK PEPPER

1 LARGE ONION, FINELY
CHOPPED

8 GARLIC CLOVES, MINCED

1 TEASPOON GROUND CUMIN

½ TEASPOON DRIED OREGANO

2 JALAPEÑOS, HALVED,
SEEDED, AND MINCED

1½ POUNDS TOMATILLOS,
HUSKED AND CHOPPED

1 CUP LOW-SODIUM CHICKEN
BROTH (USE GLUTEN-
FREE, IF NECESSARY) OR
WATER

SLICED RADISHES, PICKLED
JALAPEÑOS, LIME
WEDGES, SOUR CREAM,
AND CILANTRO LEAVES,
FOR SERVING

Think of this pleasantly tangy and comforting salsa verde–stewed chicken as a building block for a number of different dishes: You can add cooked hominy to turn it into a pozole, serve it with rice and beans, or wrap it in warm tortillas for tacos or enchiladas. Even healthier is to spoon the pulled chicken over sweet strands of roasted spaghetti squash, a healthy alternative to other kinds of starch. Because the dish is so basic, it's important to season and brown the chicken well. Also, I like to set out the dish with lots of garnishes so people can tinker to taste.

POTLUCK PREP. The pulled chicken can be refrigerated for up to 3 days. Reheat gently on the stovetop or in a 350°F oven. You can prepare this recipe through the second step and transfer everything to a slow cooker; cook on high for about 2 hours. Pull the chicken and serve it right from the cooker.

In a large enameled cast-iron Dutch oven or large pot, heat the oil over medium-high heat, swirling the pan to coat the bottom. Season the chicken generously with salt and lightly with pepper. Add enough chicken thighs to the pot so the pieces can be in an even layer without touching and cook, turning once, until very browned and crusty all over, 6 to 10 minutes. Transfer to a plate. Repeat with the remaining chicken. (You may have to do 3 or 4 batches; while time-consuming, this step makes all the difference in the flavor of the dish.)

Add the onion to the pot and cook over medium heat, stirring and loosening up any browned bits on the bottom of the pot, until the onion is softened and just starting to brown, about 8 minutes. Add the garlic and cook until just starting to soften, 1 to 2 minutes. Add the cumin, oregano, and jalapeños and cook until fragrant, about 1 minute. Add the tomatillos and broth and scrape up any remaining browned bits on the bottom of the pot, then cover and cook, stirring occasionally, until the tomatillos are broken down and saucy, about 5 minutes.

Nestle the chicken in the sauce and cover the pot. Braise the chicken over medium-low heat until the meat is cooked through and starts to pull apart with a fork, about 20 minutes. Using tongs or a slotted spoon, transfer the chicken to a bowl. Using 2 forks or your fingers, pull the meat into large chunks, discarding any large pieces of fat.

Meanwhile, if you would like the liquid to be thicker, bring it to a boil and reduce it to your liking. Return the chicken to the sauce, season again with salt and pepper, and serve with sliced radishes, pickled jalapeños, lime wedges, sour cream, and cilantro leaves.

ON BROWNING

In a wonderful piece for *Saveur* magazine, titled "In Praise of Schmutz and Schnibbles," chef and cookbook author Amy Thielen writes about how great cooks understand the power of browning and know that time obsessing over the bottom of the pan is time well spent.

"I love, for example, when the mahogany edges of a pan-fried steak leave an imprint on the pan, or the seared scallop wears an espresso-colored crown, or when that bit of chopped garlic shrinks in the sizzling oil like a gold star about to burn out, its flavor fully exhaled into the oil," she writes. For stews or anything with a pan sauce, browning or toasting the ingredients is essential for building flavor. It's where, Thielen argues, the soul of a dish lies.

If you're an impatient cook who wants to rush a dish along, maybe make something other than a stew. Otherwise, blast some of your favorite tunes, get comfy at the stove, and discover the Zen of waiting for a boneless chicken thigh to go from pale and limp to golden and crusty.

SLOW-ROASTED LEMON-SOY-HONEY PORK SHOULDER

GLUTEN-FREE (OPTIONAL) / SERVES 12 TO 20

1 (8- TO 9-POUND) BONE-IN PORK BUTT

½ CUP FRESH LEMON JUICE (FROM 4 TO 6 LEMONS)

½ CUP FRESH ORANGE JUICE (FROM 3 TO 4 ORANGES)

8 GARLIC CLOVES, MINCED

1 TABLESPOON KOSHER SALT

3 TABLESPOONS LOW-SODIUM SOY SAUCE (USE GLUTEN-FREE, IF NECESSARY)

2 TABLESPOONS GRAPESEED OIL

2 TABLESPOONS HONEY

This is the dish to make if you want an impressive hunk of meat that's not served cold. Since bone-in pork shoulder is so huge and cooks for such a long time, it holds its heat well for at least 1 hour after you pull it out of the oven. The garlicky-citrusy marinade is inspired by *pernil*, the Puerto Rican roast pork, but the honey-soy glaze gives it a slightly Asian bent. This makes the dish quite versatile, as the meat can be used in tacos or served over rice with Asian garnishes.

Arrange the pork butt in a nonreactive baking dish, fat side up. Using the tip of a sharp knife, score the fat in a crosshatch pattern.

In a medium bowl, whisk the lemon juice and orange juice with the garlic, salt, 1 tablespoon of the soy sauce, and the oil, whisking until the salt dissolves. Pour the marinade over the pork and rub it into the meat. Refrigerate for 24 to 36 hours, turning the pork a few times.

Bring the pork to room temperature for 1 to 2 hours, and then preheat the oven to 300°F.

Wipe the marinade and garlic bits off the pork and discard any excess marinade. If you plan to roast the pork in the same pan, clean it well or the sugars from the citrus will burn. Set the pork in a roasting pan fat side up.

Roast for about 3 hours. Use a spoon to baste the pork with the juices and roast for another 3 to 4 hours, basting it every hour or so, until the pork pulls easily and an instant-read thermometer inserted into the thickest part registers at least 180°F. (The cooking time will depend on how large your roast is and how well your oven returns to temperature after you baste.) Increase the oven temperature to 400°F.

In a small bowl, mix the honey with the remaining 2 tablespoons of soy sauce and brush it all over the pork. Roast for about 5 minutes. Brush the pork again and roast for 5 to 7 more minutes, until the fat is deeply browned and crisp. Let the roast stand for 30 minutes before serving, covering loosely with foil if the kitchen is chilly. Slice or use tongs to pull the meat to serve.

POTLUCK PREP. The roasted pork can stand at room temperature for at least 2 hours. If it's done cooking before it's ready to serve, you can hold it in a warm oven (about 200°F) for a few hours.

PORK AND KIMCHI SOUP
WITH TOFU AND BOK CHOY

SERVES 8 TO 12

- 1 QUART CABBAGE KIMCHI WITH LIQUID
- 3 TABLESPOONS GRAPESEED OIL OR OTHER NEUTRAL OIL
- 2 POUNDS BONELESS PORK SHOULDER, CUT INTO 1-INCH PIECES
- 1 TABLESPOON BROWN SUGAR
- 1 QUART CHICKEN STOCK OR LOW-SODIUM BROTH

- 1 TO 3 TABLESPOONS GOCHUJANG (KOREAN CHILI PASTE; AVAILABLE AT KOREAN MARKETS AND OTHER ASIAN MARKETS)
- 1 POUND FIRM SILKEN TOFU, CUT INTO ¾-INCH PIECES
- 1 LARGE HEAD BOK CHOY (NOT BABY BOK CHOY), GREEN LEAVES SEPARATED FROM THE WHITE STEMS, BOTH THINLY SLICED CROSSWISE

- 2 TEASPOONS TOASTED SESAME OIL
- SOY SAUCE, FOR SEASONING
- KOSHER SALT
- DARK GREEN PARTS OF SCALLIONS, THINLY SLICED ON THE DIAGONAL, FOR GARNISH
- STEAMED RICE, FOR SERVING (OPTIONAL)

Based on a Korean comfort soup known as *jigae*, this is the ultimate dish for a cold and rainy day. It's not a traditional version by any means, but it's satisfying—spicy and nourishing, rich and healthy, all at once. Because kimchi can vary so much, you'll need to use a little intuition as you cook. For example, if your kimchi yields less than 1 cup liquid, you might want to increase the amount of broth. And since kimchi is both salty and spicy, it's best to hold off adding too much salt and gochujang, the Korean chili paste, until the end.

This dish is somewhere between a soup and a stew, with lots of pork chunks in a thin, flavorful broth. If you'd like a thicker broth, add 2 tablespoons rice flour after you caramelize the kimchi. Alternatively, you can serve this over rice.

Set a large sieve or other strainer over a bowl. Add the kimchi and let stand, stirring occasionally, for 10 minutes, so the juice drips into the bowl; reserve the juice.

Meanwhile, in a large heavy pot or enameled cast-iron Dutch oven, heat the oil over medium-high heat. Add half of the meat in a single layer and cook, turning as necessary, until deeply golden brown all over, about 8 minutes. Transfer the browned pieces to a plate. Repeat with the remaining meat.

To the same pot set over medium-high heat, add the drained kimchi and the brown sugar and cook, stirring and scraping up browned bits from the bottom of the pan, until the kimchi is quite dry and darkens slightly, about 15 minutes. Add the kimchi juice and the chicken stock, scraping up any remaining browned bits, and then stir in 1 tablespoon of the gochujang. Return the pork and any accumulated juices to the pot and cover. Reduce the heat to low and simmer until the pork is very tender, 1 hour to 90 minutes.

Add the tofu, bok choy stems, and sesame oil to the pot and cook until the stems are crisp-tender. Season the stew with more gochujang, the soy sauce, and the salt, if necessary. Stir in the dark green bok choy leaves. Serve in bowls or over rice, garnishing with the sliced scallions.

POTLUCK PREP. The recipe can be prepared through the cooking of the meat and refrigerated for up to 3 days. Reheat gently, and add the tofu and bok choy within 1 hour or so of serving. At a potluck, you can serve this from a large slow cooker. If you want the bok choy leaves to remain vibrantly green, serve them on the side, telling people to add them, along with the scallion greens, when they ladle out their serving.

PUMPKIN BEER–AND–TURKEY CHILI
WITH BUTTERNUT SQUASH AND BEANS

SERVES 8 TO 12

8 WHOLE DRIED CHILES
(SUCH AS 4 GUAJILLO
AND 4 PASILLA, BUT YOU
COULD ALSO USE ANCHO
OR NEW MEXICO)

3 CUPS LOW-SODIUM
CHICKEN BROTH OR
WATER

¼ CUP EXTRA-VIRGIN
OLIVE OIL

1 VERY LARGE ONION,
FINELY CHOPPED

4 LARGE GARLIC CLOVES,
THINLY SLICED

KOSHER SALT

2 POUNDS GROUND TURKEY
(PREFERABLY DARK MEAT)
OR PORK

1 POUND PEELED BUTTERNUT
SQUASH, CUT INTO
BITE-SIZE PIECES
(ABOUT 4 CUPS)

¼ CUP TOMATO PASTE

2 TEASPOONS GROUND
CUMIN

1 TEASPOON COCOA POWDER

2 (12-OUNCE) BOTTLES
PUMPKIN ALE OR
BROWN ALE

½ CUP APPLE CIDER OR JUICE

2 (15-OUNCE) CANS BLACK
BEANS, RINSED AND
DRAINED

2 (15-OUNCE) CANS PINTO
BEANS, RINSED AND
DRAINED

SOUR CREAM, CHOPPED
FRESH CILANTRO, FINELY
CHOPPED WHITE ONION,
SLICED JALAPEÑOS,
AND LIME WEDGES, FOR
SERVING

Pumpkin ale is a great addition to an autumn bowl of chili. Often brewed with brown sugar and spices, the beer lets you add multiple ingredients at once. Unlike many chilis, this one uses no fresh or canned tomatoes—only tomato paste. Most of the flavor comes from the beer and the pureed rehydrated chiles. While the chiles do add another step, they have so much more complexity and character than commercial ground chili powder. To help this chili still come together quickly, you could use peeled and pre-chopped butternut squash.

In a dry medium skillet, toast the chiles over medium heat, turning occasionally with tongs, until warm and fragrant, about 2 minutes. Let cool to touch.

Rip the stems off the chiles and dump out the seeds; rip the chiles into pieces if necessary to remove every seed. Put the chiles in a medium saucepan and add the broth. Bring to a boil over high heat. Remove the pan from the heat and let stand until the chiles are very soft, about 30 minutes. Transfer the chiles and the liquid to a blender or food processor and puree.

Meanwhile, in a large, heavy pot or enameled cast-iron Dutch oven, heat the olive oil over medium heat. Add the onion and garlic, season generously with salt, and cook, stirring occasionally, until the onion is translucent, about 8 minutes.

(RECIPE CONTINUES)

Add the ground meat, increase the heat to medium-high, and cook, breaking it up with a spoon, until it is opaque throughout and browned in spots. Add the squash, tomato paste, and cumin and cook until the tomato paste starts to coat the bottom of the pan and the cumin is fragrant, 1 to 2 minutes. Add the cocoa powder and pumpkin ale and bring to a boil. Add the apple cider, the chile puree, and the beans and bring to a boil.

Reduce the heat to medium-low and simmer until the chili is thick and flavorful, about 40 minutes. (The chili will seem quite spicy when you first add the puree but the heat will mellow as it cooks.)

Season with salt to taste and serve the chili hot, with the accompaniments on the side.

POTLUCK PREP. The chili can be refrigerated for up to 4 days or frozen for up to 1 month. Reheat gently on the stovetop. Serve hot, using a slow cooker if necessary. Bring the accompaniments in separate small containers for serving.

BEEF AND ROOT VEGETABLE STEW
WITH SALTY THINGS

SERVES 8 TO 12

¼ CUP PLUS 1 TABLESPOON GRAPESEED OIL

1 POUND BONELESS BEEF STEW MEAT, PREFERABLY GRASS-FED

KOSHER SALT AND FRESHLY GROUND BLACK PEPPER

3 TABLESPOONS ALL-PURPOSE FLOUR

2 MEDIUM ONIONS, CHOPPED (ABOUT 2 CUPS)

4 GARLIC CLOVES, THINLY SLICED

¼ CUP TOMATO PASTE

1 TEASPOON GROUND ALLSPICE

2 QUARTS WATER

2 BAY LEAVES

1 SMALL CELERY ROOT (ABOUT 1 POUND), PEELED WITH A KNIFE AND CUT INTO BITE-SIZE PIECES (ABOUT 2 CUPS)

½ POUND CARROTS (6 SMALL TO MEDIUM), CUT INTO BITE-SIZE PIECES (ABOUT 2 CUPS)

½ POUND PARSNIPS (2 MEDIUM), CUT INTO BITE-SIZE PIECES (ABOUT 2 CUPS)

½ POUND KIELBASA, QUARTERED LENGTHWISE AND CUT INTO BITE-SIZE PIECES

1 CUP SAUERKRAUT

2 SOUR PICKLES, QUARTERED AND SLICED ¼ INCH THICK (1 CUP)

1½ TABLESPOONS DRAINED CAPERS

¼ CUP PITTED BLACK OLIVES, PREFERABLY MOROCCAN OIL-CURED, THINLY SLICED

SOUR CREAM, LEMON SLICES, AND CHOPPED FRESH DILL OR FLAT-LEAF PARSLEY, FOR SERVING

Some people head out to Brighton Beach, a Brooklyn neighborhood where immigrants from former Soviet countries have settled, for the pierogis. I go for the soleyanka, a soup that proves "mystery meat" can be an awesome thing. I love this soup because you never know what you'll get on your spoon. Yes, there are all kinds of sausages but also olives, capers, and pickles. For this version, I retained the salty things but cut back on the amount of meat, adding some nourishing root vegetables instead. The kielbasa, beef, and tomato paste still give the broth such an incredible rich and smoky flavor that I don't miss the other sausages.

In a large enameled cast-iron Dutch oven or heavy pot, heat 3 tablespoons of the oil over medium-high heat, swirling the pan to coat the bottom. In a large bowl, season the beef very lightly with salt and pepper and toss with the flour. Add half the beef to the pan in a single layer so the pieces aren't touching and cook over medium-high heat, turning once or twice, until the pieces are well browned, 6 to 8 minutes. Transfer to a plate. Repeat with the remaining beef.

Add the remaining 2 tablespoons oil. Add the onions and garlic, and cook until softened, about 8 minutes. Add the tomato paste and cook until it starts to coat the bottom of the pan and darkens,

(RECIPE CONTINUES)

about 2 minutes. Add the allspice and cook until fragrant, about 30 seconds. Add the water and bay leaves and bring to a boil. Reduce the heat to medium-low, cover partially, and simmer for 1 hour. Add the celery root, carrots, parsnips, kielbasa, and sauerkraut; cover completely and cook until the vegetables are tender, about 1 hour longer. Add the pickles, capers, and olives and cook until heated through. Taste the soup; if it seems too salty to you, add just a little more water to adjust the seasoning.

Ladle the stew into bowls and top with sour cream, lemon slices, and dill, and serve.

POTLUCK PREP. The stew can be refrigerated for up to 3 days. Reheat gently before serving and serve from the stovetop or a slow cooker.

SPICED BEEF AND LAMB MEATBALLS

MAKES ABOUT 32 SMALL MEATBALLS

FOR THE TOMATO SAUCE

- 2 (28-OUNCE) CANS WHOLE TOMATOES
- 2 TABLESPOONS EXTRA-VIRGIN OLIVE OIL
- 2 MEDIUM ONIONS, FINELY CHOPPED
- KOSHER SALT
- 1 TO 2 TABLESPOONS HARISSA (OPTIONAL; AVAILABLE AT SPECIALTY SHOPS)
- 1 TABLESPOON HONEY (OPTIONAL)

FOR THE MEATBALLS

- 1 POUND GROUND LAMB
- 1 POUND GROUND BEEF, PREFERABLY GRASS-FED AND 80% LEAN
- 1 CUP DRY BREAD CRUMBS
- 2 TABLESPOONS MINCED GARLIC (ABOUT 4 CLOVES)
- 2 LARGE EGGS
- ¼ CUP FINELY CHOPPED FRESH FLAT-LEAF PARSLEY
- ¼ CUP FINELY CHOPPED FRESH MINT
- 1 TABLESPOON GROUND CORIANDER
- 1 TABLESPOON SWEET PAPRIKA
- 2 TEASPOONS GROUND CUMIN
- ½ TEASPOON GROUND CINNAMON
- 2½ TEASPOONS KOSHER SALT
- FRESHLY GROUND BLACK PEPPER
- ¼ CUP EXTRA-VIRGIN OLIVE OIL
- ½ POUND FETA CHEESE, CRUMBLED
- 2 CUPS CHOPPED FRESH HERBS, SUCH AS CILANTRO, PARSLEY, MINT, AND DILL

Meatballs are a great party food—super comforting and filling, if a little mono-lithic. I wanted to create meatballs that were familiar and tender but also dynamic, tasting of warm spices, salty cheese, and a confetti of mixed herbs. I added harissa, too, which gives the sauce a kick, but you can leave it out for a milder flavor.

If you plan to double the recipe and don't want to spend the time frying the meatballs, you can roast them: Preheat the oven to 450°F. Spread the meatballs in a single layer on 1 or 2 parchment-lined baking sheets, and roast until well browned, 15 to 20 minutes. (See photograph on pages 90–91.)

POTLUCK PREP. You can refrigerate the cooked meatballs in the sauce for up to 2 days. Reheat gently and serve from the stovetop or a slow cooker. Bring the crumbled cheese and herbs in separate containers, along with small spoons to allow guests to garnish the meatballs themselves.

MAKE THE TOMATO SAUCE: If you don't have an immersion blender, puree the tomatoes in a food processor before making the sauce.

In a heavy pot, heat the olive oil over medium heat. Add the onions, season with salt, and cook, stirring occasionally, until the onions are translucent, about 8 minutes. Add 1 tablespoon of the harissa (if desired) and cook until fragrant, about 1 minute. Add the tomatoes or tomato puree and the honey. (If you have an immersion blender, turn off the heat and use the blender to puree the tomatoes.)

Bring the sauce to a simmer, reduce the heat to medium-low, and cook, stirring occasionally, until the sauce is thickened and tastes very cooked, about 40 minutes. Add more harissa if desired, season with salt, and keep warm.

MEANWHILE, MAKE THE MEATBALLS: Line a baking sheet or a large platter with parchment paper.

In a large bowl, use your hands to vigorously mix the ground meat with the bread crumbs, garlic, eggs, parsley, mint, coriander, paprika, cumin, cinnamon, salt, and a few grinds of pepper. Using lightly moistened hands, roll the mixture into small balls (about 2 tablespoons each), and then transfer to the prepared baking sheet.

In a large skillet, heat the olive oil over medium-high heat. Add as many meatballs as you can fit in a single layer without them touching and cook, turning them frequently, until nicely browned all over, about 5 minutes. Transfer to a clean plate. Repeat with the remaining meatballs.

Add all of the meatballs to the sauce, cover, simmer over medium-low heat until cooked through, about 8 minutes. Serve hot, sprinkled with feta and herbs.

THE 9×13-INCH PAN

CASSEROLES & THE LIKE

ANNA'S SUMMER VEGETABLE TIAN

VEGAN; GLUTEN-FREE / MAKES ONE 9 × 13-INCH TIAN

5 TABLESPOONS EXTRA-VIRGIN OLIVE OIL

1 GARLIC CLOVE, HALVED

1 RED BELL PEPPER, STEMMED, CORED, AND THINLY SLICED

1 MEDIUM RED ONION, HALVED AND THINLY SLICED

KOSHER SALT AND FRESHLY GROUND BLACK PEPPER

¼ CUP CHOPPED FRESH BASIL, OR 2 TABLESPOONS FRESH THYME LEAVES, PLUS MORE FOR GARNISH

1 MEDIUM EGGPLANT (ABOUT 12 OUNCES), SLICED ¼ INCH THICK

9 SMALL RED TOMATOES (ABOUT 1 POUND), CORED AND SLICED ¼ INCH THICK

2 MEDIUM OR 1 LARGE ZUCCHINI (ABOUT 12 OUNCES), SLICED ¼ INCH THICK

I discovered Anna Watson Carl and her awesome blog and cookbook, both called *The Yellow Table*, the way many people discover each other these days: through Instagram. I love (and share!) her passions for France and for bringing people together around a table. When I asked her about contributing a recipe, she immediately said she wanted to do a classic Provençal tian. "It's perfect because you can serve it hot or at room temperature," she said. "Plus, it actually tastes better made a day ahead." A tian is a fairly rustic vegetable bake, but to make it as pretty as possible, Anna advises buying eggplant, zucchini, and tomatoes that are about the same width. (See photograph on page 110.)

POTLUCK PREP. The whole baked tian or the leftovers can be refrigerated for up to 3 days. Serve warm or at room temperature.

Grease a 9 × 13-inch baking dish with 1 tablespoon of the olive oil. Rub the sides of the dish with the garlic.

In a large, nonstick skillet, heat 2 tablespoons olive oil over medium-high heat. Swirl the garlic in the pan for 1 to 2 minutes or until fragrant; discard the garlic. Add the red pepper and onion and cook, stirring frequently, until beginning to soften, 5 minutes. Reduce the heat to medium and continue cooking, stirring occasionally, until extremely soft, 7 to 8 more minutes. Season with salt and pepper, and remove from the heat. Stir in half of the chopped basil and let cool slightly.

Preheat the oven to 425°F.

Spread the pepper-onion mixture in the bottom of the baking dish. Arrange the remaining vegetables so they're standing up in the dish in 3 long rows, repeating the following pattern: 1 eggplant slice, 1 tomato slice, and 1 zucchini slice. Season the vegetables generously with salt and pepper, sprinkle with the remaining chopped basil, and drizzle with the remaining 2 tablespoons olive oil.

Cover the baking dish with foil and bake for 30 minutes. Remove the foil and bake for 30 more minutes, or until the vegetables are beginning to brown. Let cool slightly and serve.

SAMOSA-FILLING STUFFED POBLANOS

VEGAN (OPTIONAL); GLUTEN-FREE / MAKES 16 SMALL OR 8 LARGE STUFFED CHILES

- 2 LARGE BAKING POTATOES (ABOUT 1½ POUNDS TOTAL), PEELED AND CUT INTO 1-INCH PIECES
- 2 TABLESPOONS COCONUT OIL, GHEE (SIMILAR TO CLARIFIED BUTTER), OR UNSALTED BUTTER, PLUS MELTED COCONUT OIL, GHEE, OR BUTTER, FOR RUBBING AND DRIZZLING
- 1 TEASPOON CUMIN SEEDS
- 1 TEASPOON CORIANDER SEEDS

- ¼ CUP MINCED SHALLOTS (ABOUT 1 LARGE SHALLOT)
- 1 (1-INCH) PIECE FRESH GINGER, PEELED AND MINCED
- 1 SERRANO CHILE, SEEDED AND MINCED
- KOSHER SALT AND FRESHLY GROUND BLACK PEPPER
- ½ CUP FROZEN PEAS, THAWED
- 1 TABLESPOON FRESH LEMON JUICE

- ½ TEASPOON GARAM MASALA
- 8 SMALL POBLANO CHILES (ABOUT 1½ OUNCES EACH), OR 4 LARGE (ABOUT 4 OUNCES EACH)
- MINT OR CILANTRO LEAVES, FOR GARNISH
- GREEN CHUTNEY (PAGE 226, OR STORE-BOUGHT; OPTIONAL), FOR SERVING
- DAIRY YOGURT OR COCONUT MILK YOGURT (OPTIONAL), FOR SERVING

Samosas are one of my favorite Indian snacks; these fried dough pockets are stuffed with a spiced potato filling and served with a mix of sauces. I use a similar filling for these chiles, which add a satisfying heat to the dish. Without the accompaniments, the chiles end up looking quite humble, but they are more delicious than they appear to be. (In fact, whenever people taste them, they request the recipe.) To make them look as good as they taste, choose a few different accompaniments. In addition to those listed in the recipe, you can also sprinkle the chiles with chaat masala or drizzle with tamarind chutney, both of which are available at Indian markets.

In a medium saucepan, cover the potatoes with water and bring to a boil. Simmer over medium-high heat until tender, about 10 minutes. Drain well and wipe out the saucepan.

In the same saucepan, melt the 2 tablespoons of coconut oil over medium-high heat. Add the cumin and coriander seeds, and cook until they pop, 30 seconds to 1 minute. Add the shallots, ginger, serrano chile, and a pinch of salt, and cook until golden, 2 to 4 minutes. Remove the pan from the heat, add the potatoes, and lightly mash them so no large chunks remain. Stir in the peas, lemon juice, and garam masala, and season with salt and pepper.

Preheat the oven to 375°F. Lightly oil a 9 × 13-inch baking dish.

(RECIPE CONTINUES)

Halve the poblanos lengthwise and use scissors to snip out the cores and seeds. Lightly rub the chiles with some of the oil and season the insides with salt. Arrange the chiles cut side up in a 9 × 13-inch baking dish. Scoop the filling into the chile halves and dot or drizzle with a little more oil. Cover the dish with foil.

Bake for 10 minutes. Remove the foil and bake for 20 to 30 more minutes (the larger chiles take longer to cook), until softened. Garnish with the herbs and serve hot or at room temperature with Green Chutney and yogurt, if desired.

POTLUCK PREP. The filling can be refrigerated for up to 3 days. The assembled stuffed chiles can be refrigerated overnight. Bake at the host's house or transport hot or at room temperature. The stuffed chiles can stand at room temperature for about 2 hours.

LATE-SUMMER VEGETABLE ENCHILADA PIE

VEGETARIAN; GLUTEN-FREE / SERVES 8 TO 16

FOR THE SAUCE

1½ OUNCES ANCHO CHILES
(2 TO 3)

1 CUP BOILING WATER

1 (28-OUNCE) CAN WHOLE
TOMATOES

KOSHER SALT AND
FRESHLY GROUND
BLACK PEPPER

FOR THE FILLING AND PIE

2 TABLESPOONS EXTRA-
VIRGIN OLIVE OIL

1 MEDIUM ONION, FINELY
CHOPPED (ABOUT 1½ CUPS)

2 GARLIC CLOVES, MINCED

2 JALAPEÑOS, SEEDED AND
FINELY CHOPPED

2 TEASPOONS MILD CURRY
POWDER

1 POUND ZUCCHINI OR
OTHER SUMMER SQUASH,
CUT INTO ¼-INCH PIECES
(ABOUT 4 CUPS)

2 MEDIUM EARS OF CORN,
KERNELS CUT FROM THE
COBS (ABOUT 1½ CUPS)

1¾ CUPS COOKED BLACK OR
PINTO BEANS, OR
1 (15-OUNCE) CAN,
DRAINED

1 TABLESPOON FRESH LIME
JUICE

½ CUP FRESH CILANTRO
LEAVES, ROUGHLY
CHOPPED, PLUS MORE FOR
GARNISH

12 (6- TO 7-INCH) CORN
TORTILLAS

1¼ POUNDS MONTEREY JACK
CHEESE, GRATED
(5 TO 6 CUPS)

I always love looking for the overlap in ingredients between different cuisines. For example, both Mexican food and Indian food rely on flavorful, warmly spiced sauces; they use a variety of vegetables and legumes; and they include flatbreads at many meals. As a nod to this overlap, I included curry powder in this otherwise straightforward enchilada pie—a saucy, lasagna-like American dish that pretends to be Mexican. Despite the use of chiles, the casserole is fairly mild. If you'd like more heat, leave in some or all of the jalapeño seeds.

MAKE THE SAUCE: In a large, deep skillet, toast the anchos over medium-high heat, turning frequently, until fragrant, about 2 minutes. When they're cool enough to handle, stem the chiles and shake out the seeds, ripping the chiles if you have to. Transfer the chiles to a blender (or a cup that's heat-safe if your blender jar is not) and cover with the boiling water; let stand until softened and cooled. Add the tomatoes and blend until smooth. Season with salt and pepper.

MAKE THE FILLING AND ASSEMBLE THE PIE: In the same skillet used to toast the anchos, heat the olive oil over medium heat. Add the onion and cook, stirring, until softened, about 5 minutes.

(RECIPE CONTINUES)

Add the garlic and jalapeños and cook until fragrant and softened, about 2 minutes. Add the curry powder and cook until fragrant, 1 minute. Add the zucchini and cook, stirring, until tender but not mushy, about 5 minutes. Add the corn and beans and cook, mashing the beans slightly, until hot, about 2 minutes. Remove the filling from the heat and stir in the lime juice and ½ cup of the cilantro.

Preheat the oven to 375°F. Grease a 9 × 13-inch baking dish.

Spread a thin layer of sauce in the bottom of the pan (about ½ cup). Arrange one-third of the tortillas in the baking dish, tearing them in half as necessary to create an even layer. Spoon half of the filling over the tortillas and top with one-third of the cheese. Top the cheese with another layer of tortillas, followed by half of the remaining sauce, the rest of the filling, and another one-third of the cheese. Finally, layer

more tortillas, followed by the remaining sauce and the remaining cheese.

Bake for about 30 minutes, until the filling is bubbling and the edges are starting to brown. Let cool for 10 minutes, and then serve.

POTLUCK PREP. The sauce and the filling can be refrigerated separately for up to 3 days. The assembled enchilada pie can be refrigerated overnight. You can bake at the host's house or transport hot as directed on page 18.

SMOKY SQUASH MAC & CHEESE

VEGETARIAN; GLUTEN-FREE / SERVES 6 TO 12

1 (3-POUND) WINTER
SQUASH, SUCH AS RED
KURI, ACORN, BUTTERNUT
OR KABOCHA, HALVED
AND SEEDED

OLIVE OIL, FOR BRUSHING

KOSHER SALT AND
FRESHLY GROUND
BLACK PEPPER

UNSALTED BUTTER,
FOR THE PAN

2 CUPS WHOLE MILK

1 POUND EXTRA-SHARP
CHEDDAR CHEESE, HALF
FRESHLY GRATED (ABOUT
1¼ CUPS) AND HALF
CUT INTO SMALL CUBES
(ABOUT ⅛ INCH)

4 OUNCES SMOKED GOUDA,
FRESHLY GRATED
(ABOUT 1¼ CUPS)

1 POUND GLUTEN-FREE CORN
ELBOW MACARONI OR
FUSILLI

1½ OUNCES PARMIGIANO-
REGGIANO CHEESE,
FRESHLY GRATED
(ABOUT ½ CUP)

There's a myth that gluten-free food has to be virtuous. That's not so. This mac & cheese is as gooey and cheesy and as indulgent as ever, with its campfire edge coming from the smoked Gouda. I've chosen to add squash and corn macaroni because they taste great together, and the squash also happens to thicken the sauce, so you don't have to add flour. If you can't find corn noodles, you can substitute any macaroni or fusilli, gluten-free or not. I love red Kuri squash here, which has a chestnut flavor and lends a vivid orange color that reminds me of mac & cheese from the box.

Preheat the oven to 400°F. Brush the cut sides of the squash with olive oil, season with salt and pepper, and put on a baking sheet cut sides down. Roast the squash for about 40 minutes, until very tender all the way through. Let cool slightly.

Reduce the oven temperature to 350°F. Butter a 9 × 13-inch baking dish.

Scoop 3 cups of the squash out of the skin into a large saucepan set over medium heat; if you have any remaining squash, reserve it for another use. Add the milk to the saucepan and heat to warm.

Using a potato masher or whisk, mash the squash until smooth; alternatively, if you want a silkier consistency, you can puree the squash with an immersion blender or transfer the mixture to a blender to puree. Add the grated cheddar and Gouda to the saucepan and cook, stirring occasionally, until the cheese has melted, 5 to 6 minutes. Keep the sauce warm, stirring occasionally as necessary.

(RECIPE CONTINUES)

Meanwhile, in a large pot of boiling salted water, cook the macaroni until not quite al dente (likely 3 minutes shy of the cooking time suggested on the box). Reserve 1 cup of the cooking water, and then drain.

Add the pasta to the cheese sauce and stir until well coated, adding pasta water if necessary to loosen the sauce. (The sauce will thicken in the oven, so if you like a loose, creamy mac & cheese, definitely add some water.) Stir in the cubed cheddar cheese, and then pour the mixture into the prepared baking pan. Sprinkle the Parmigiano all over the top.

Bake for about 30 minutes, until the cheese sauce is bubbling and some of the Parmesan cheese is browned. (If you'd like a super golden-brown layer, pop the mac & cheese under the broiler for about 3 minutes.) Let cool for about 15 minutes before serving.

POTLUCK PREP. The assembled mac & cheese can be refrigerated overnight. Bake at the host's house or transport the hot casserole as directed on page 18.

NO-NOODLE LASAGNA
WITH MUSHROOM BOLOGNESE AND RICOTTA

VEGETARIAN; GLUTEN-FREE / MAKES ONE 9 × 13-INCH LASAGNA

FOR THE MUSHROOM BOLOGNESE

- 1 OUNCE DRIED PORCINI MUSHROOMS
- 1½ CUPS BOILING WATER
- 1 SMALL ONION, COARSELY CHOPPED
- 2 MEDIUM CARROTS, COARSELY CHOPPED
- 1 POUND KING TRUMPET MUSHROOMS (ALSO KNOWN AS KING OYSTER MUSHROOMS), COARSELY CHOPPED
- ¼ CUP EXTRA-VIRGIN OLIVE OIL

- KOSHER SALT AND FRESHLY GROUND BLACK PEPPER
- ½ CUP DRY RED WINE
- 1 CUP STORE-BOUGHT TOMATO PUREE (OR PUREED CANNED TOMATOES)
- 1 SMALL RIND OF PARMIGIANO-REGGIANO CHEESE
- 1 TEASPOON MINCED FRESH ROSEMARY

FOR THE CELERY ROOT NOODLES AND RICOTTA FILLING

- 1 LARGE CELERY ROOT (AT LEAST 1½ POUNDS)
- KOSHER SALT
- 2 POUNDS FRESH RICOTTA
- 8 OUNCES FONTINA CHEESE, SHREDDED (ABOUT 2 CUPS)
- 4 OUNCES PARMIGIANO-REGGIANO, FRESHLY GRATED (ABOUT 2 CUPS)
- FRESHLY GROUND PEPPER, PREFERABLY WHITE
- 2 LARGE EGGS, BEATEN
- UNSALTED BUTTER, FOR THE PAN

This recipe is a blend of two smart ideas. The first—using sliced celery root as "noodles"—comes from Sarah Britton, of the terrific blog *My New Roots*. The second is the deeply flavorful mushroom bolognese, which is based on a recipe I edited from Chicago chef Sarah Grueneberg. When those ideas are combined with a classic ricotta filling, you get lasagna that's rich but not overwhelmingly so and one that's as good at room temperature as it is hot. The bolognese relies on king trumpet mushrooms because they

hold their meaty texture even after they're cooked. If you can't find them, substitute white button mushrooms, or use 4 cups of your favorite bolognese.

POTLUCK PREP. The lasagna can be assembled and refrigerated overnight. You can cook it right from the fridge; just add a few minutes to the cooking time. Bake at the host's house or transport the hot lasagna as directed on page 18.

MAKE THE MUSHROOM BOLOGNESE: In a bowl, cover the porcini mushrooms with the boiling water and let stand while you prepare the vegetables.

In a food processor, process the onion, carrots, and mushrooms until finely chopped, about 30 pulses. In a large pot, heat the olive oil over medium heat. Add the vegetables, season with salt and pepper, and cook until softened, about 20 minutes.

Drain the porcini and reserve the soaking liquid. Rinse and finely chop the porcini, and then add them to the vegetables. Cook until fragrant, about 10 minutes. Add the wine, bring to a boil, and cook until reduced by half, about 3 minutes. Add the tomato puree, porcini soaking liquid, and Parmigiano rind. Reduce the heat to medium-low and simmer, partly covered, until thickened. Discard the cheese rind, stir in the rosemary, and remove from the heat.

PREPARE THE CELERY ROOT NOODLES AND RICOTTA FILLING: Using a very sharp knife, peel the celery root. Using the knife or a mandoline, slice the celery root into thin slabs, between ⅛ and ¼ inch thick. (If your celery root is very large, it helps to halve it or trim it to a rectangular piece.) The goal is to get thin pieces that you will layer like noodles in lasagna. While they don't all have to be the same size, you should aim for even thickness.

In a medium saucepan, bring 1 inch of water to a boil and season well with salt. Add the celery root, cover, and steam, stirring a few times, until the thickest piece is tender, about 3 minutes; drain.

In a large bowl, mix the ricotta with half of the fontina and Parmigiano cheeses and season with salt and pepper. Beat in the eggs with a wooden spoon.

Preheat the oven to 375°F. Butter a 9 × 13-inch glass or ceramic dish.

Spread a thin layer of the mushroom sauce in the pan (about ½ cup) and arrange half the celery root on top, overlapping the pieces slightly so they form a layer. Spread half the remaining sauce on top, followed by half the ricotta. Top with the remaining celery root, followed by the remaining sauce and the remaining ricotta.

In a bowl, toss the remaining Parmigiano cheese with the remaining fontina, and sprinkle on the top of the lasagna.

Bake for 40 to 45 minutes, until the top is golden and crisp around the edges. Let the lasagna stand for 20 minutes before serving. (If you'd like a super golden top, pop the lasagna under the broiler for a few minutes.)

POLENTA STUFFED WITH SAUSAGE AND BROCCOLI RABE

GLUTEN-FREE / SERVES 6 TO 10

- 4 TABLESPOONS (½ STICK) UNSALTED BUTTER, PLUS MORE FOR THE PAN
- 7 CUPS WATER
- KOSHER SALT
- 2 CUPS MEDIUM-GRIND POLENTA OR CORNMEAL

- 4 OUNCES PARMIGIANO-REGGIANO CHEESE, FINELY GRATED (ABOUT 2 CUPS)
- 1 LARGE BUNCH BROCCOLI RABE (ABOUT 1 POUND), HALVED CROSSWISE
- 2 TABLESPOONS EXTRA-VIRGIN OLIVE OIL

- 2 GARLIC CLOVES, MINCED
- 1 POUND SWEET ITALIAN SAUSAGE (LOOSE MEAT OR SQUEEZED FROM ITS CASINGS)
- 1 POUND PROVOLONE CHEESE SLICES

The classic Italian American sandwich of sausage and broccoli rabe inspired this over-the-top stuffed polenta. Broccoli rabe is notoriously bitter, but here, the greens are cooked with the sausage long enough that the flavor mellows. I tried using "fancier" cheeses in this dish, but I loved how slices of provolone become melty in the oven and stretchy when you slice the polenta.

POTLUCK PREP. The assembled stuffed polenta can be refrigerated overnight. Bake at the host's house or transport the hot casserole as directed on page 18.

Butter a 9 × 13-inch baking dish.

In a large pot, bring the water to a boil. Add 2 teaspoons salt, and then slowly whisk in the polenta. Reduce the heat to medium-low and simmer the polenta, stirring frequently until tender and creamy, about 20 minutes. Add the 4 tablespoons of butter and about one-third of the Parmigiano cheese, and stir to melt.

Ladle 3 cups of the polenta into the prepared baking dish and spread into an even layer. Refrigerate until firm while you make the filling.

In a deep skillet, bring 1 inch of salted water to a boil. Add the broccoli rabe, cover, and simmer over medium heat, stirring a few times, until bright green and just barely tender, 2 to 3 minutes. Drain the broccoli rabe in a colander and run under cold water to cool. Use your hands to squeeze the leaves as dry as you can. Transfer the broccoli rabe to a food processor and pulse several times to finely chop, or finely chop with a knife.

(RECIPE CONTINUES)

Wipe out the skillet and heat the olive oil over medium-high heat. Add the sausage meat, increase the heat to high, and cook, breaking up the meat with a spoon, until cooked through and browned in spots, about 5 minutes. Add the garlic and cook until fragrant and softened, about 1 minute. Reduce the heat to medium, add the greens, and cover the skillet. Cook, stirring occasionally and scraping up any browned bits on the bottom of the pan, until the greens stop releasing water and are very soft, about 7 minutes. Add another one-third of the Parmigiano and cook until it melts; remove from the heat.

Preheat the oven to 375°F.

Take the baking pan out of the refrigerator and layer about half of the provolone slices on top of the polenta, tearing pieces as necessary to make a single layer. Spread the broccoli rabe and sausage filling in an even layer on top of the provolone. Arrange another layer of provolone slices on top. (You may have a few slices left over.)

Gently rewarm the remaining polenta, adding ¼ cup or so of water to loosen if necessary. Spoon or pour the warmed polenta over the provolone and spread into an even layer. Sprinkle the remaining Parmigiano over the top of the casserole.

Bake for about 35 minutes, until the filling is bubbling and the cheese is browned. Let rest for about 10 minutes before serving.

PORK-STUFFED COLLARDS
WITH TOMATO SAUCE

GLUTEN-FREE / MAKES 12 TO 16 STUFFED COLLARDS

1 TABLESPOON UNSALTED
BUTTER

1 SMALL ONION, FINELY
CHOPPED

KOSHER SALT

1 CUP RED OR BROWN
SHORT-GRAIN RICE

1½ POUNDS COLLARD GREENS

1 POUND GROUND PORK

½ TEASPOON GROUND
ALLSPICE

ZEST OF 1 SMALL ORANGE

FRESHLY GROUND BLACK
PEPPER

SIMPLE TOMATO SAUCE
(RECIPE FOLLOWS)

If you've never been to Veselka, the famous Ukrainian restaurant in New York's East Village, after a night out, you absolutely have to go. The borscht is a lifegiving hangover cure and the stuffed cabbage is the most perfect thing you can eat on a subfreezing night. These stuffed greens are loosely inspired by Veselka's stuffed cabbage. I flavor the meat-and-rice filling with a little allspice and orange zest, and use pleasantly bitter collard greens in place of the cabbage leaves.

In a medium saucepan, heat the butter over medium heat. Add the onion and ¼ teaspoon salt, and cook until very soft, about 8 minutes. Add the rice and stir to coat. Add 1½ to 2 cups water (check the package directions of the rice for the best guide) and bring to a boil. Cover, reduce the heat to medium-low, and simmer until the rice is tender. Let cool to room temperature.

Meanwhile, bring a large saucepan of generously salted water to a boil. Add the collard greens and cook, in batches if necessary, until bright green, about 3 minutes. Transfer them to a cutting board and let cool. Trim off any tough stems and thick ribs, and pick out the 12 largest leaves or 16 medium to small leaves to use for stuffing. Finely chop the remaining leaves.

In a large bowl, combine the cooled rice with the pork, the chopped collards, the allspice, orange zest, 1½ teaspoons salt, and a few grinds of pepper.

Preheat the oven to 375°F.

(RECIPE CONTINUES)

Working with one collard leaf at a time, arrange about ⅓ cup filling in the center of the larger leaves or ¼ cup filling in the smaller leaves. Fold the stem end over the filling, and then tuck in the sides. Roll the collard over to form a bundle, overlapping the ends to seal. Transfer, seam side down, to a 9 × 13-inch baking dish. Repeat with the remaining ingredients. Pour the tomato sauce over the stuffed leaves and cover the pan.

Bake for about 30 minutes, until the sauce is bubbling and the leaves are tender. Serve hot or warm.

POTLUCK PREP. The assembled stuffed collards can be refrigerated overnight. The cooked stuffed collards can be reheated gently in a 300°F oven.

SIMPLE TOMATO SAUCE
MAKES ABOUT 2 CUPS

1 (28-OUNCE) CAN WHOLE TOMATOES
2 TABLESPOONS EXTRA-VIRGIN OLIVE OIL
1 SMALL ONION, FINELY CHOPPED
    PINCH OF RED PEPPER FLAKES
    KOSHER SALT

If you don't have an immersion blender, puree the tomatoes in a food processor.

In a saucepan, heat the olive oil over medium heat. Add the onion and red pepper flakes, and cook, stirring occasionally, until the onion is very soft, about 8 minutes. Add the tomatoes and use an immersion blender to puree the mixture, then bring to a boil. Reduce the heat to moderate and simmer, stirring occasionally, until slightly thickened, about 20 minutes. Season with salt and serve.

PHOEBE'S MOROCCAN-INSPIRED SHEPHERD'S PIE

GLUTEN-FREE / SERVES 6 TO 10

2 POUNDS POTATOES (ABOUT 3 SMALL TO MEDIUM RUSSETS), PEELED AND CUT INTO 1-INCH PIECES

1 POUND CARROTS (8 MEDIUM), PEELED AND CUT INTO ½-INCH PIECES

SEA SALT AND FRESHLY GROUND BLACK PEPPER

2½ TABLESPOONS FRESH LEMON JUICE

¼ CUP PLUS 2 TABLESPOONS OLIVE OIL

1 LARGE VIDALIA OR OTHER SWEET ONION, CHOPPED

1½ POUNDS GROUND LAMB

2 GARLIC CLOVES, MINCED

1 TEASPOON GROUND CUMIN

1 TEASPOON SWEET PAPRIKA

2 TABLESPOONS TOMATO PASTE

1 TABLESPOON HARISSA

1 BUNCH WINTER GREENS (ABOUT ¾ POUND CHARD OR TENDER KALE), FINELY CHOPPED WITH STEMS

1 CUP BEEF STOCK OR WATER

2 TABLESPOONS CHOPPED FRESH CILANTRO, PLUS MORE FOR GARNISH

Phoebe Lapine, who writes the blog *Feed Me Phoebe,* is one of my absolute favorite recipe developers. Her food is always familiar with a twist, and she has a knack for making comfort food that just so happens also to be healthy. Here, she created a delicious shepherd's pie. She says: "My mom is the queen of both shepherd's pie and Moroccan lamb tagine. When I fled the nest, these two things haunted my home-cooked comfort-food dreams more than anything else. I've created my own versions of each over the years, but it wasn't until recently that I thought of combining them by adding tons of Moroccan spices and harissa to the pie's lamb filling. Since my philosophy is to eat a lot of good with a little bad, I also added kale to the base and carrots to the mash, which offsets the earthy spices with a nice sweetness. I think my mother would be proud."

POTLUCK PREP. The assembled casserole can be refrigerated overnight. Bake at the host's house or transport the hot casserole as directed on page 18.

Preheat the oven to 350°F.

In a large pot, cover the potatoes and carrots with water and generously season with salt. Bring to a boil and simmer until the vegetables are fork-tender, 10 to 15 minutes. Drain, reserving 1 cup of the liquid. Return the vegetables to the pot and mash until semi-smooth. (It's okay if they are a little chunky, but if you prefer a more even texture and color, pass the mash through a food mill.) Whisk in the lemon juice, ¼ cup olive oil, and enough cooking liquid to reach your desired consistency (adding it 1 tablespoon at a time). Season with salt and set aside.

Meanwhile, in a large, deep skillet, heat the remaining 2 tablespoons olive oil over medium-high heat. Add the onion, season lightly with salt and pepper, and cook until softened, about 5 minutes. Push the onion to the side of the pan, increase the heat to high, and add the lamb. Season the meat lightly with salt and cook, breaking it apart with the back of a spoon, until browned and cooked through, about 10 minutes. Add the garlic, cumin, paprika, tomato paste, and harissa. Cook until the spices are very fragrant and the tomato paste coats the bottom of the pan, about 2 minutes. Stir in the greens, cover, and cook until wilted, about 3 minutes. Pour in the stock, scraping up any brown bits that may have formed on the bottom of the pan. Simmer until reduced by half. Remove from the heat and stir in the cilantro. Season with more salt and pepper, if necessary. Scrape the lamb filling into a 9 × 13-inch baking dish. Spread the carrot-potato mash on top.

Bake for about 25 minutes, until the filling is bubbling and the top has formed a slight crust. Garnish with cilantro and serve hot.

HEALTHY ROOT VEGETABLE GRATIN
WITH BUTTERY WALNUTS

VEGETARIAN (OPTIONAL); GLUTEN-FREE / SERVES 8 TO 12

- 2½ POUNDS SWEET POTATOES, PEELED
- 1 LARGE CELERY ROOT (2 POUNDS), PEELED WITH A SHARP KNIFE AND HALVED LENGTHWISE
- 1 MEDIUM RUTABAGA (2 POUNDS), PEELED AND HALVED LENGTHWISE

- ½ TABLESPOON UNSALTED BUTTER, MELTED, PLUS MORE FOR THE PAN
- KOSHER SALT AND FRESHLY GROUND BLACK PEPPER
- 1 CUP LOW-SODIUM CHICKEN OR VEGETABLE BROTH

- ¼ CUP HEAVY CREAM
- 1½ CUPS WALNUTS
- 1 TEASPOON ROUGHLY CHOPPED FRESH THYME LEAVES

My former co-worker at *Food & Wine*, Melissa Rubel-Jacobsen, is a genius cook, and she showed me how gratins don't need to be thick with cream and cheese to be delicious. All you need are some flavorful root vegetables. This recipe is based on one she created for *Food & Wine*, but instead of using her bread-crumb topping, I sprinkle herbed walnuts on top. The process of thinly slicing the vegetables is admittedly time-consuming, but I promise that the results are worth the effort. A mandoline makes the job even easier.

POTLUCK PREP. The assembled gratin can be refrigerated overnight. To keep the nuts from getting soft, I like to sprinkle them on just before serving. While you can transport the gratin in an insulated carrier and serve it hot, it's also terrific at room temperature.

Using a mandoline or a very sharp knife, slice the potatoes lengthwise into slabs that are about ⅛ inch thick. Halve the celery root and the rutabaga and slice each into ⅛-inch-thick slabs.

Preheat the oven to 375°F. Butter a 9 × 13-inch glass or ceramic baking dish.

Arrange one-third of the sweet potatoes in the dish, overlapping them slightly; season with salt and pepper. Top with half the rutabaga, and then half the celery root, seasoning each layer. Repeat the layering, ending with a third layer of sweet potatoes. Pour the broth over and around the vegetables. Cover the baking dish tightly with foil.

Bake for about 45 minutes, until the vegetables are almost tender when pierced. Remove the foil and pour the cream over the gratin. Bake for 30 minutes, until the liquid has thickened.

Meanwhile, spread the walnuts on a baking sheet and toast in the oven for about 4 minutes, until fragrant. Let cool, and then coarsely chop. Return the chopped walnuts to the baking sheet, toss with the ½ tablespoon of butter and the thyme, and season with salt and pepper. Toast the nuts until nicely browned, about 2 minutes.

Remove from the oven and top with the walnuts. Let stand for 10 minutes. Serve hot, warm, or at room temperature.

EGG CASSEROLE
WITH SPAGHETTI SQUASH, MUSHROOMS, GOAT CHEESE, AND DILL

VEGETARIAN; GLUTEN-FREE / SERVES 6 TO 12

UNSALTED BUTTER, FOR THE PAN

1 MEDIUM SPAGHETTI SQUASH (2 TO 3 POUNDS), HALVED AND SEEDED

¼ CUP EXTRA-VIRGIN OLIVE OIL, PLUS MORE FOR BRUSHING

KOSHER SALT AND FRESHLY GROUND BLACK PEPPER

6 GARLIC CLOVES, UNPEELED

1 POUND WHITE BUTTON MUSHROOMS OR A MIX OF WILD MUSHROOMS, SLICED ¼ INCH THICK

12 LARGE EGGS, LIGHTLY BEATEN

½ CUP CRÈME FRAÎCHE

½ CUP FRESH DILL, FINELY CHOPPED

1 (4-OUNCE) PACKAGE FRESH GOAT CHEESE, CRUMBLED

I created this casserole for my dad, who in recent years has cut back on starchy breakfasts in favor of those rich in protein and vegetables. He is picky about the vegetables he likes, and these are a couple of his favorites. The spaghetti squash blends into the eggs to the point that you barely know it's there; it just adds a gentle sweetness and some bulk. If you prefer, you can leave it out.

POTLUCK PREP. You can roast the squash and garlic and cook the mushrooms up to 2 days in advance. Refrigerate them in separate containers. Then, you can refrigerate the assembled, unbaked casserole the night before and bake it in the morning. The casserole can stand at room temperature for up to 4 hours.

Preheat the oven to 400°F. Line a large rimmed baking sheet with parchment paper. Generously butter a 9 × 13-inch baking dish.

Brush the cut sides of the squash with olive oil, season with salt and pepper, and set on the prepared baking sheet. Brush the garlic with olive oil and add to the squash. Roast for about 40 minutes, until the squash is tender when pierced with a fork. Let cool slightly, and then use a fork to rake the squash into threads.

Reduce the oven temperature to 325°F.

In a large, deep skillet, heat ¼ cup of olive oil over medium heat. Add the mushrooms, stir, and season lightly with salt. Cover and cook until the mushrooms start to release their liquid, about 3 minutes. Uncover and cook until the mushrooms are browned, about 5 minutes longer. Add the spaghetti squash to the pan and cook until it starts to brown in spots and stick to the pan, 5 minutes. Let cool.

In a large bowl, whisk the eggs with the crème fraîche and ¼ teaspoon salt until smooth. Squeeze the roasted garlic into the bowl and whisk in as well. Stir in the vegetables, the dill, and cheese. Pour into the prepared baking pan.

Bake for 30 to 40 minutes, until just set in the center. Let cool, and then cut into squares. Serve warm or at room temperature.

SUPPORTING-ROLE SALADS & SIDES

MANY BEAN SALAD
WITH TENDER HERBS, CHILES, WALNUTS, AND LEMON

VEGAN; GLUTEN-FREE / SERVES 8 TO 16

3 OUNCES WALNUTS (ABOUT ¾ CUP)

2 LEMONS

8 OUNCES FRESH GREEN BEANS, TRIMMED AND CUT INTO 1-INCH PIECES

8 OUNCES FRESH WAX BEANS, TRIMMED AND CUT INTO 1-INCH PIECES

1 TO 2 LARGE JALAPEÑOS, STEMMED, SEEDED, AND FINELY CHOPPED (OPTIONAL)

1 MILD RED CHILE, SUCH AS ANAHEIM OR HOLLAND, STEMMED, SEEDED, AND FINELY CHOPPED (OPTIONAL)

2 TEASPOONS PURE MAPLE SYRUP OR HONEY

3 CUPS COOKED SHELL BEANS (SEE PAGE 141), SUCH AS CRANBERRY BEANS, CHICKPEAS, BLACK-EYED PEAS, BLACK BEANS, PINTO BEANS, OR ANY HEIRLOOM VARIETIES, OR 2 (14-OUNCE) CANS BEANS OF CHOICE

½ CUP EXTRA-VIRGIN OLIVE OIL

1 LIGHTLY PACKED CUP TENDER FRESH HERBS (MY FAVORITE COMBINATION IS ⅔ CUP CILANTRO, ⅓ CUP DILL)

KOSHER SALT AND FRESHLY GROUND BLACK PEPPER

After working on a story about Georgian food (the country, not the state), that region's combination of cilantro, chiles, and walnuts stuck with me. Georgians are also big fans of bean salads, so it made sense to look to the country's food when updating the classic American bean salad.

I like to add at least two types of shell beans along with the green beans and wax beans. If you have the time, it's worth shelling fresh beans or cooking high-quality dried beans (for more about cooking both fresh and dried beans, see page 141). Of course, if you're short on time, canned beans work just fine, too.

Preheat the oven or toaster oven to 350°F.

Spread the walnuts on a baking sheet and toast for about 5 minutes, until golden and fragrant. Let cool slightly, and then coarsely chop. (Alternatively, you can toast them on the stovetop in a dry skillet, stirring frequently.)

Using a sharp knife, remove the rind and bitter white pith from one of the lemons. Cut in between the membranes to release the sections onto a cutting board, and then finely chop the flesh, removing any seeds. Squeeze the juice from the membranes into a measuring cup. Squeeze the juice from the remaining lemon into the measuring cup. (You should have about ¼ cup of juice total.)

In a medium saucepan or deep skillet, bring 1 inch of salted water to a boil. Add the green beans and cook until just tender, 6 to 8 minutes.

(RECIPE CONTINUES)

Using a slotted spoon, transfer them to a colander and cool under cold water. Add the wax beans to the boiling water and cook until tender, 4 to 6 minutes. Transfer them to same colander and cool under cold water.

In a large bowl, mix the lemon juice with the chopped lemon, the jalapeños and other chile, and maple syrup. Add the green beans, wax beans, shell beans, and olive oil and toss. Stir in the walnuts and the herbs, season with salt and pepper, and refrigerate for at least 1 hour and up to 6 hours. Season again with salt and lemon juice before serving.

POTLUCK PREP. The steamed green and wax beans and any cooked beans can be refrigerated overnight. The dressed salad without the herbs holds up nicely for a few hours in the refrigerator. While you can keep the salad overnight, the flavors aren't as vibrant the next day. As with any food that's been chilled, taste and re-season it with salt and lemon juice before serving.

ON BEANS

Canned beans are convenient, but fresh shell beans and good-quality dried beans have much better flavors and textures. If you eat beans regularly and usually opt for canned, I highly recommend you up your game.

SHELL BEANS

If you have the time (or can con a toddler into helping you), it's worth shelling fresh beans when they're in season (usually late summer into early fall). The flavor of fresh beans is unmatched.

To end up with 3 cups cooked beans, start with about 3 pounds beans in the pod. Pick out pods that look as unblemished as possible, with beans that look plump through the pod. Shell the beans and cook them in a pot of salted simmering water until tender and creamy, 20 to 40 minutes depending on the size and freshness of the bean. Add crushed garlic, bay leaves, and other herbs to the water for flavor.

Refrigerate the cooked beans in their cooking liquid for up to 3 days, or freeze them for up to a month. You can also refrigerate shelled uncooked beans for about 1 week.

DRIED BEANS

For years, I avoided cooking dried beans because they'd simmer for hours and never get as tender and creamy as they should have. My mistake? Buying poor-quality supermarket beans. Over the last decade, companies like Rancho Gordo (ranchogordo.com) and Community Grains (communitygrains.com), as well as many small farms, have started selling both standard and heirloom varieties of beans. These beans are more expensive, but they're also fresher (often dried within the last year), so you'll rarely have a bad batch.

To Soak or Not to Soak? After lots of experimentation, I've become a dedicated bean soaker. Yes, you can cook them without soaking, but I have found that the texture is less even. People also swear that soaking beans makes them more digestible.

To soak, just cover them with at least 2 inches of water and leave them for up to 8 hours at room temperature, or refrigerate for up to 48 hours. Drain off the water and cook.

If you want to soak the beans but are in a bit of a hurry, you can also cover the beans with at least 1 inch of water, bring to a boil, turn off the heat, and let stand for 1 hour; then drain.

Cooking Dried Beans. To end up with about 3 cups cooked beans, start with 1 cup dried beans. After soaking, cover the beans with at least 2 inches of water, add a large pinch of salt, and bring to a boil. After the water boils for a few minutes, reduce the heat to medium-low, bring down to a simmer, and skim off any foam that forms on the top. Add a crushed garlic clove, a bay leaf, and sturdy herb sprigs, if you like. Then cover the pot partially and simmer them until tender. The cooking time will depend on a number of factors, including the variety and freshness of the beans. Start checking them after 45 minutes. They're done when they're so tender that they're creamy but not mushy and falling apart (unless you're making a puree). Add more water as needed. Season with more salt, if desired.

Cooking dried beans in the pressure cooker is magic; it cuts the cooking time by more than half. If you have one, try it out (use the manufacturer's instructions). I guarantee you'll never go back to canned beans.

The cooked beans can be refrigerated in their liquid (which is incredibly tasty itself) for up to 3 days, or frozen for about 1 month.

CITRUS AND BITTERS SALAD

VEGAN; GLUTEN-FREE / SERVES 8 TO 12

½ CUP PLUS 2 TABLESPOONS EXTRA-VIRGIN OLIVE OIL

2 SMALL HEADS RADICCHIO (ABOUT 1¼ POUNDS TOTAL), QUARTERED

KOSHER SALT AND FRESHLY GROUND BLACK PEPPER

2 LARGE WHITE OR PINK GRAPEFRUITS

1 LARGE CARA CARA ORANGE OR NAVAL ORANGE

3 LARGE CELERY STALKS, SLICED ¼ INCH THICK ON THE DIAGONAL

1 LARGE FENNEL BULB, QUARTERED, CORED, AND SLICED CROSSWISE ¼ INCH THICK

1 CUP FRESH FLAT-LEAF PARSLEY LEAVES, COARSELY CHOPPED

2 TABLESPOONS SHERRY VINEGAR

1 TABLESPOON PURE MAPLE SYRUP

½ CUP TOASTED WALNUTS, COARSELY CHOPPED

Once people embrace crunchy bitter salads like this one, I find they begin to crave them. This salad is especially good on the cusp between winter and spring, when everyone is sick of eating root vegetables. Thankfully, that's when a lot of these ingredients hit their peak season. If you'd like an extra-salty hit here, add some black olives or feta cheese.

In a large skillet, heat 2 tablespoons of the olive oil over medium-high heat. Season the radicchio quarters with salt and pepper and add them to the skillet with one of the flat sides down. Cook, turning, until all sides are well browned, 2 to 3 minutes per side. Transfer to a work surface and let cool.

Meanwhile, using a sharp knife, peel the grapefruits and orange, removing all of the bitter white pith. Cut in between the membranes to release the sections into a large bowl.

Thinly slice the radicchio leaves crosswise, avoiding the cores. Add the shredded radicchio, the celery, fennel, and parsley, and toss gently.

In a small bowl, whisk the sherry vinegar with the maple syrup, and gradually whisk in the remaining ½ cup olive oil.

Just before serving, drizzle the dressing over the salad and toss. Add the toasted walnuts and toss again.

POTLUCK PREP. The salad and the dressing can be prepared and refrigerated separately overnight. Bring to room temperature before serving. The dressed salad will stand at room temperature for about 1 hour.

CUCUMBER SALAD
WITH CREAMY POPPY SEED DRESSING

VEGETARIAN; GLUTEN-FREE / SERVES 8 TO 10

1½ POUNDS SEEDLESS
CUCUMBERS, SLICED AS
DESIRED, OR STANDARD
CUCUMBERS, PEELED IF
WAXED, HALVED, SEEDED,
AND SLICED AS DESIRED

KOSHER SALT

½ CUP CRÈME FRAÎCHE OR
SOUR CREAM

1 TABLESPOON FRESH LEMON
JUICE

½ TEASPOON FRESHLY
GRATED LEMON ZEST

¼ CUP ROUGHLY CHOPPED
FRESH HERBS, SUCH
AS MINT, DILL, AND
TARRAGON, PLUS MORE
FOR GARNISH

1 TABLESPOON CHOPPED
FRESH CHIVES, PLUS
MORE FOR GARNISH

1 TEASPOON POPPY SEEDS

This simple salad is fairly close to the traditional recipes for a creamy cucumber salad, but it's brightened with more herbs and has a pleasant crunch, thanks to the poppy seeds. If you like, you can also add thinly sliced raw sugar snap peas or snow peas, or lightly cooked sweet English peas to the salad; just throw them in soon before serving so they don't lose their vibrant green color.

In a strainer set over a bowl, toss the cucumbers with ½ teaspoon salt and let stand for 1 hour. Discard any water that drains out of the cucumbers.

In a large bowl, whisk the crème fraîche with the lemon juice and lemon zest. Whisk in the herbs and poppy seeds. Add the cucumbers and stir until the vegetables are coated with the dressing. Refrigerate for at least 30 minutes; stir again, then season with salt and garnish with more herbs before serving.

POTLUCK PREP. The cucumber salad can be refrigerated for about 6 hours and is best served lightly chilled. To keep it cold, serve it in an insulated bowl or a chilled ceramic bowl.

MARINATED TOMATOES
WITH ZA'ATAR

VEGETARIAN; GLUTEN-FREE / SERVES 6 TO 10

1 TABLESPOON WHITE WINE VINEGAR

½ TEASPOON HONEY

2 TABLESPOONS EXTRA-VIRGIN OLIVE OIL

2 POUNDS RIPE TOMATOES, CORED AND CUT INTO 1-INCH WEDGES (OR HALVED OR QUARTERED CHERRY TOMATOES)

1 SMALL RED ONION, THINLY SLICED (OPTIONAL)

2 TEASPOONS ZA'ATAR, HOMEMADE (PAGE 223) OR STORE-BOUGHT

KOSHER SALT AND FRESHLY GROUND BLACK PEPPER

This super-simple tomato salad calls for za'atar, a Middle Eastern blend of dried herbs, toasted sesame seeds, and sumac, a tart powder made from a dried berry. It's fantastic served alongside Spiced Butterflied Lamb with Date Barbecue Sauce (page 83) or slices of grilled bread. Because the tomatoes get so juicy, you might want to serve them with a slotted spoon.

In a large bowl, whisk the vinegar with the honey and olive oil. Add the tomatoes, red onion, and za'atar and gently stir until the tomatoes are coated with the dressing. Season with salt and pepper and let stand at room temperature, stirring a few times, for 30 minutes before serving.

POTLUCK PREP. You can refrigerate the dressed tomatoes for up to 8 hours. Serve lightly chilled or at room temperature. The tomatoes can stand at room temperature for at least 2 hours. Smaller tomatoes will hold up best over time.

WHIPPED HERB RICOTTA
WITH SUMMER TOMATOES

VEGETARIAN; GLUTEN-FREE (EXCEPT THE TOASTS FOR SERVING) / SERVES 8 TO 16

2 POUNDS FRESH
WHOLE-MILK RICOTTA
(ABOUT 4 CUPS)

¼ CUP PLUS 2 TABLESPOONS
EXTRA-VIRGIN OLIVE
OIL, PLUS MORE FOR
DRIZZLING

½ CUP MIXED CHOPPED
FRESH HERBS, SUCH AS
CHIVES, BASIL, MINT,
AND/OR TARRAGON

KOSHER SALT AND
FRESHLY GROUND
BLACK PEPPER

2 POUNDS MIXED RIPE
HEIRLOOM TOMATOES,
CUT INTO ⅛-INCH PIECES
(ABOUT 6 CUPS; CHERRY
TOMATOES CAN BE
HALVED OR QUARTERED)

TOASTS OR FLATBREAD,
FOR SERVING (OPTIONAL)

There is nothing wrong with a good tomato-mozzarella salad, but I prefer piling chopped tomatoes over milky whipped ricotta and serving it in the center of a table with some toasts for spreading and dipping. The dish eventually becomes quite messy, with the tomato juices mixing with the ricotta, but that's what I love about it.

Please try to avoid the usual supermarket ricotta for this recipe—it's grainy rather than creamy. Instead, look for freshly made ricotta (even better if you can find sheep's milk versions) from cheese shops, specialty food shops (including Whole Foods), or farmers' markets. I whip it by hand, but if you'd like to make it really airy and smooth, you can whip it in your food processor, electric mixer, or stand mixer. (See photograph on pages 136–137.)

Chill a medium platter or large shallow serving bowl for at least 30 minutes.

In a large bowl, beat the ricotta with ¼ cup of the olive oil until fluffy, about 2 minutes. Fold in half of the herbs and season generously with salt and pepper.

In another bowl, gently stir the tomatoes with the remaining 2 tablespoons olive oil. Add the remaining herbs, season with salt and pepper, and stir again.

Spoon the whipped ricotta into the prepared platter or bowl, making a shallow well in the center. Spoon the tomatoes into the well, drizzle with a little more olive oil, and serve with toasts or flatbread.

POTLUCK PREP. The whipped ricotta can be refrigerated overnight. The assembled dish can be refrigerated for about 2 hours. Serve lightly chilled or at room temperature; it can stand at room temperature for about 90 minutes.

VEGAN CAPRESE SALAD

VEGAN; GLUTEN-FREE / SERVES 8 TO 16

4 (15-OUNCE) CANS CANNELLINI BEANS (OR 6 CUPS COOKED BEANS FROM ABOUT 2½ CUPS DRIED), RINSED AND DRAINED

4 GARLIC CLOVES

2 BAY LEAVES

1 TABLESPOON FINELY CHOPPED LEMONGRASS (FROM 1 STALK, OPTIONAL)

¼ CUP EXTRA-VIRGIN OLIVE OIL, PLUS MORE FOR DRIZZLING

KOSHER SALT AND FRESHLY GROUND BLACK PEPPER

4 POUNDS MIXED RIPE TOMATOES, SLICED INTO ROUNDS OR WEDGES

FLAKY SALT, FOR GARNISH

BASIL LEAVES, TORN, FOR GARNISH

This version of Caprese, made with an olive-oil–rich bean salad, was originally intended for the vegan (or dairy-free) friends in your life, but it's so good that omnivores will love it, too.

The keys here are using great tomatoes (of course), along with a healthy amount of olive oil and salt. Inspired by a salad I found while flicking through Patricia Wells's *The Provence Cookbook,* I added a little lemongrass to the beans. If lemongrass is difficult to find, leave it out; the dish is still great without it.

In a medium pot, combine the beans with the garlic and bay leaves. Cover with water and simmer over medium-low heat until the beans lose some of the canned flavor, 15 to 20 minutes. Drain well and discard the garlic and bay leaves.

In a bowl, gently toss the beans with the lemongrass and ¼ cup olive oil; they will fall apart a bit and that's okay. Season generously with salt and a few grinds of pepper.

Spoon the beans onto a platter and arrange the tomatoes on top. Drizzle with more olive oil and garnish with flaky salt, basil, and a few more grinds of pepper, then serve.

POTLUCK PREP. You can bring the salad already assembled to a potluck—the tomato juices will flavor the beans. I prefer to add the basil just before serving to make sure it doesn't darken. The bean salad can be refrigerated overnight. Bring to a cool room temperature before serving; it can stand at room temperature for up to 2 hours.

GRILLED CORN SALAD
WITH LIME MAYO, CILANTRO, AND RADISHES

VEGETARIAN; GLUTEN-FREE / SERVES 8 TO 16

8 MEDIUM TO LARGE EARS
OF CORN

2 TEASPOONS MINCED
SHALLOT

½ CUP FRESH LIME JUICE
(FROM 4 TO 6 LIMES)

¼ CUP MAYONNAISE

1 TEASPOON SMOKED
PAPRIKA (SWEET OR HOT)

½ CUP CRUMBLED OR
SHREDDED COTIJA CHEESE
OR QUESO BLANCO

8 MEDIUM RADISHES,
HALVED AND THINLY
SLICED

1½ CUPS FRESH CILANTRO
LEAVES, ROUGHLY
CHOPPED

KOSHER SALT

This smoky, crowd-pleasing salad is inspired by the Mexican street snack of corn on the cob slathered with mayonnaise and cheese, known as *elote*. The hefty dose of lime juice, which balances the sweetness of the corn, will keep people coming back for more.

If you don't have a grill (or a grill pan), you can boil the ears of corn. Just try not to substitute frozen kernels, which tends to be less milky than corn freshly cut from the cob.

Light a grill or preheat a grill pan. Pull back the corn husks but leave them attached; remove and discard all of the silks. Fold the husks back up over the corn. Grill the corn over moderately high heat, turning occasionally, until the husks are well browned and black in spots and the corn is very hot, about 10 minutes. Transfer to a platter and let cool.

Meanwhile, in a large bowl, mix the shallot with the lime juice and let stand for 5 minutes. Whisk in the mayonnaise and paprika.

Using a serrated knife, cut the corn from the cobs (you should have about 8 cups kernels). Add the corn and the cheese to the dressing and toss. Within 1 hour of serving, add the radishes and cilantro, season with salt, and serve.

POTLUCK PREP. The salad without the radishes and cilantro can be made earlier in the day and refrigerated. It can stand at room temperature for up to 2 hours.

RED CABBAGE SLAW
WITH PICKLES AND CARAWAY

VEGAN; GLUTEN-FREE / SERVES 6 TO 12

1 TEASPOON CARAWAY
SEEDS

½ CUP CIDER VINEGAR

2 HALF-SOUR DELI PICKLES,
HALVED LENGTHWISE
AND THINLY SLICED INTO
HALF-MOONS (ABOUT
1 CUP)

¼ CUP PICKLE BRINE

1½ TABLESPOONS SUGAR

1 (2-POUND) HEAD RED
CABBAGE, CORED AND
FINELY SHREDDED
(ABOUT 12 CUPS)

KOSHER SALT

With antioxidant-rich red cabbage and naturally fermented pickles and brine, this crisp, tangy slaw is incredibly healthy. But that's not why you should make it. It also happens to be delicious, especially when served alongside rich meat dishes, like summer barbecue and winter braises. While the slaw is good an hour after it's made, it's especially tasty when left to marinate for a day or two in the fridge. If you prefer, you can substitute a head of green cabbage or about 12 cups of shredded cabbage or coleslaw mix. (See photograph on page 148.)

In a small skillet, toast the caraway seeds over moderate heat until fragrant, about 1 minute. Transfer to a small bowl or mortar, and then use a pestle or the bottom of an ice cream scoop to lightly crush the seeds.

In a large bowl, whisk the vinegar with the pickle brine and sugar. Add the cabbage, caraway seeds, and pickles and toss. Season with salt and refrigerate for at least 1 hour, tossing occasionally. Toss well before serving.

POTLUCK PREP. The slaw can be refrigerated for up to 3 days and can stand at room temperature for at least 2 hours.

KIMCHI AND KALE "CAESAR"

VEGAN (OPTIONAL) / SERVES 6 TO 8

- 2 CUPS CABBAGE KIMCHI, DRAINED OF EXCESS LIQUID
- ½ CUP MAYONNAISE (VEGAN MAYO IS FINE)
- ¼ CUP FRESH LEMON JUICE
- 2 POUNDS TUSCAN KALE (LACINATO OR DINOSAUR KALE), STEMS REMOVED AND LEAVES FINELY CHOPPED CROSSWISE
- 6 CUPS BITE-SIZE PIECES COUNTRY BREAD (FROM ABOUT 6 SLICES)
- ¼ CUP EXTRA-VIRGIN OLIVE OIL
- KOSHER SALT

When I first tasted this dressing of mayonnaise, lemon juice, and pureed kimchi—a spicy Korean pickle—I was shocked at how Caesar-like it is. I guess I shouldn't be surprised—the kimchi itself has a lot of the same components, including plenty of garlic, anchovy, and just a general funk that mimics Parmesan cheese. (You can substitute fish-less kimchi if you can find it.) Also, like many kale salads, this one is best when left to marinate for at least an hour and will even hold up overnight.

In a food processor, pulse the kimchi with the mayonnaise and lemon juice until you have a coarse puree.

In a large bowl, toss the dressing with the kale and refrigerate for at least 1 hour.

Meanwhile, preheat the oven to 375°F. On a large baking sheet, toss the bread with the olive oil and bake for 10 to 15 minutes, until golden. Let cool.

Season the salad with salt, if necessary. Add the croutons, toss, and serve.

POTLUCK PREP. The dressed kale salad without the croutons can be refrigerated overnight. The cooled croutons can be kept in an airtight container overnight. Add them to the salad within 1 hour of serving. The salad can be served chilled or at room temperature and can stand at room temperature for 2 hours.

POTATO SALADS FOR FOUR SEASONS

As long as it's seasoned well, I like most types of potato salad, even that yellowish scoopable type you see at the deli counter. Potato salads are potluck classics. Here, I've reimagined them to fit different seasons.

GREEN THINGS AND POTATO SALAD

VEGAN; GLUTEN-FREE / SERVES 6 TO 12

After months and months of root vegetables in the Northeast, we're all craving green vegetables. The salad might seem a bit fussy, asking you to boil and ice-water–shock the vegetables separately, but it's worth it. To turn this salad into a main course, you could serve some quartered hard-boiled eggs alongside.

1 TEASPOON FINELY CHOPPED SHALLOT

2 TABLESPOONS FRESH LEMON JUICE, PLUS MORE FOR SEASONING

1 TEASPOON DIJON MUSTARD

3 TABLESPOONS EXTRA-VIRGIN OLIVE OIL

1 POUND FINGERLING POTATOES, SCRUBBED

KOSHER SALT AND FRESHLY GROUND BLACK PEPPER

1 POUND ASPARAGUS, ENDS TRIMMED; SPEARS CUT INTO 1-INCH LENGTHS

½ POUND SUGAR SNAP PEAS, TRIMMED AND STRINGED IF NECESSARY, HALVED CROSSWISE

1 CUP FROZEN PEAS

1 TABLESPOON FINELY CHOPPED FRESH TARRAGON

In a large bowl (one you could use for serving), whisk the shallot with the lemon juice and mustard. Gradually whisk in the olive oil in a thin stream.

In a medium pot of boiling water, cook the potatoes until tender when pierced with a fork, 12 to 15 minutes. Drain, and then refill the pot with water and return to a boil. Let the potatoes cool to warm, and then quarter them (or you can cut into rounds). Add the potatoes to the dressing and toss.

Set a bowl of ice water next to the stove. Salt the boiling water generously. Add the asparagus and cook until crisp tender, about 3 minutes. Use a slotted spoon to transfer it to the ice-water bath, adding more ice if necessary to keep it cold. Add the sugar snap peas to the boiling water and cook until bright green, about 1 minute. Use a slotted spoon to transfer to the ice water. Add the frozen peas and cook until hot, about 1 minute. Drain in a colander, and then transfer the peas to the ice water. When the vegetables are cool, drain and dry them well.

Within a few minutes of serving, add the vegetables and the tarragon to the potatoes and toss. Season with salt and more lemon juice, if desired, and serve.

POTLUCK PREP. While you can toss everything together well in advance, the jade vegetables will start to turn a less pretty army green soon after they hit the dressing. I prefer to bring the dressed potatoes in a serving bowl and the green vegetables with the herbs in a separate container, and toss them together just before serving. Another option is to arrange the vegetables on a platter and serve the dressing alongside. The salad can stand at room temperature for up to 2 hours.

GREEK EXPAT POTATO SALAD

VEGETARIAN; GLUTEN-FREE / SERVES 8 TO 16

In the summer, I prefer a chilled potato salad with just enough mayonnaise to make it scoopable. This one—dressed with an oregano-parsley pesto—is robustly flavored and especially good with anything grilled. The combination of oregano and lemon reminds me of Greece, but the hit of mayonnaise makes the salad feel all American—hence the name. While the salad is perfect with just the potatoes and the dressing, you can make it feel even more Greek by adding olives, feta, and/or finely chopped pepperoncini. And if you're not an oregano person, substitute the same amount of mint or 2 roughly chopped tablespoons of fresh rosemary.

3 POUNDS YUKON GOLD POTATOES

2 GARLIC CLOVES

1 PACKED CUP FRESH FLAT-LEAF PARSLEY

⅓ CUP FRESH OREGANO LEAVES

¼ CUP ROASTED ALMONDS OR TOASTED WALNUTS (ABOUT 1 OUNCE)

KOSHER SALT AND FRESHLY GROUND BLACK PEPPER

½ CUP EXTRA-VIRGIN OLIVE OIL

2 TABLESPOONS FRESH LEMON JUICE, PLUS MORE FOR SEASONING

¼ CUP MAYONNAISE

In a large pot, cover the potatoes with water and bring to a boil. Simmer over medium heat until the potatoes are tender when pierced with a fork, 15 to 20 minutes, depending on the size of the potatoes. Add the garlic cloves to the boiling water and cook just until slightly softened, about 1 minute. Drain and let cool to warm.

Place the garlic, parsley, oregano, nuts, 1 teaspoon salt, and a couple of grinds of pepper into a food processor and pulse until finely chopped. With the machine on, slowly add the oil in a thin stream. Scrape the pesto into a large bowl and stir in the lemon juice and mayonnaise.

When the potatoes are cool enough to handle, rub off the skins (if desired) and chop into ¾-inch pieces. Add the potatoes to the dressing and toss well, breaking up the potatoes slightly with the spoon. Season with salt and pepper. Serve at room temperature or chill for at least 3 hours, seasoning again with salt, pepper, and lemon juice if necessary.

POTLUCK PREP. You can serve this potato salad right from the refrigerator. To keep it cold, serve the bowl set over ice.

ROASTED RED AND SWEET POTATO SALAD WITH CANDIED BACON AND SCALLIONS

SERVES 8 TO 16

German potato salad, which my family eats at least once a year with the Christmas ham, inspired this dish. Just like the classic, it balances smoky, rich bacon with tangy vinegar. Adding sweet potatoes, miso, and candied bacon (Pig Candy, page 25) creates more layers of flavor. As they roast, the sweet potatoes become a bit softer than the red potatoes, and that's okay; when they're tossed, they break down a little bit, giving the salad a creamier texture.

8 SCALLIONS

1½ POUNDS RED-SKINNED POTATOES, CUT INTO ½-INCH PIECES

1½ POUNDS SWEET POTATOES, CUT INTO ½-INCH PIECES

¼ CUP EXTRA-VIRGIN OLIVE OIL

KOSHER SALT AND FRESHLY GROUND BLACK PEPPER

2 TABLESPOONS SHERRY VINEGAR

1 TABLESPOON MISO, PREFERABLY WHITE

6 STRIPS PIG CANDY (PAGE 25) OR COOKED BACON, CRUMBLED

Preheat the oven to 400°F.

Separate the dark green tops from the light green and white parts of the scallions. In a large bowl, toss the red and sweet potatoes and the white and light green parts of the scallions (you can leave the scallion pieces whole) with the olive oil, and season with salt and pepper. Spread the mixture out on 1 large or 2 medium baking sheets in a single layer. Roast for 30 to 40 minutes, stirring once halfway through, until tender.

Pick out the roasted scallions and transfer to a work surface. Return the potatoes to the bowl. Thinly slice the roasted scallions crosswise and add them to the potatoes. Thinly slice the dark green parts of the scallions until you have ½ cup.

In a small bowl, whisk the vinegar with the miso, drizzle over the warm potatoes, and toss. Add most of the crumbled bacon and most of the ½ cup of dark green scallions and toss again. Let stand for at least 10 minutes before serving, and then garnish with the remaining bacon and scallions.

POTLUCK PREP. The dressed potatoes with the scallions can be refrigerated overnight. Bring to room temperature and add the bacon before serving. Because of the vinegar, the scallion greens will lose their color, so garnish with fresh ones just before serving. The salad can stand at room temperature for up to 2 hours.

POTATO SALAD WITH FENNEL AND PICKLY THINGS

VEGAN; GLUTEN-FREE / SERVES 8 TO 16

If there were more room in my Twitter bio, it would definitely say, "Loves fennel and pickly things." I like to use fennel in places you'd normally find celery. Here, it adds an unexpected flavor to this tangy potato salad.

2 POUNDS FINGERLING OR OTHER SMALL POTATOES, HALVED OR SLICED ½ INCH THICK

KOSHER SALT AND FRESHLY GROUND BLACK PEPPER

2 TABLESPOONS WHITE WINE VINEGAR

1 TABLESPOON DIJON MUSTARD

⅓ CUP EXTRA-VIRGIN OLIVE OIL

1 SMALL FENNEL BULB (NOT BABY FENNEL), HALVED, CORED, AND CUT INTO BITE-SIZE PIECES (ABOUT 1½ CUPS)

8 CORNICHON PICKLES, DRAINED AND THINLY SLICED INTO ROUNDS

1 TABLESPOON MINCED PICKLED ONIONS (FROM THE CORNICHON JAR)

2 TABLESPOONS CAPERS, DRAINED AND ROUGHLY CHOPPED

½ CUP FRESH FLAT-LEAF PARSLEY LEAVES OR DILL, ROUGHLY CHOPPED

In a large saucepan, cover the potatoes with water and bring to a boil. Season the water generously with salt and simmer over medium-high heat until the potatoes are tender, 6 to 10 minutes, depending on the size of the pieces. Drain well.

Meanwhile, in a large bowl, whisk the vinegar with the mustard and olive oil. Add the warm potatoes and toss. Add the fennel, cornichons, pickled onions, and capers and toss again. Season with salt and pepper. Add the parsley within 1 hour of serving.

POTLUCK PREP. The potato salad can be refrigerated, without the parsley, overnight. Serve chilled or at room temperature; it can stand at room temperature for 2 hours.

COCONUT-ROASTED SQUASH WEDGES
WITH LEMONGRASS-SHALLOT RELISH

GLUTEN-FREE (OPTIONAL); VEGAN (OPTIONAL) / SERVES 6 TO 12

1 SMALL KABOCHA SQUASH OR MEDIUM ACORN SQUASH (ABOUT 2½ POUNDS), HALVED, SEEDED, AND CUT INTO 1-INCH-THICK WEDGES

¼ CUP PLUS 2 TABLESPOONS VIRGIN COCONUT OIL

KOSHER SALT AND FRESHLY GROUND BLACK PEPPER

½ CUP MINCED SHALLOT

¼ CUP FRESH LIME JUICE

4 LEMONGRASS STALKS

2 FRESH OR FROZEN KAFFIR LIME LEAVES, MINCED (SEE NOTE)

1 TABLESPOON PLUS 1 TEASPOON ASIAN FISH SAUCE OR SOY SAUCE (USE GLUTEN-FREE IF NECESSARY)

1 TO 3 FRESH BIRD'S EYE CHILES, THINLY SLICED, OR 1 SERRANO CHILE, HALVED AND THINLY SLICED

CHOPPED ROASTED UNSALTED PEANUTS OR CASHEWS, FOR GARNISH

SLICED SCALLION GREENS, FOR GARNISH

These squash wedges are meant to be served as large pieces that can be eaten with a fork and knife, or picked up and nibbled. The fiery, fragrant relish served alongside is based on a sauce from Bali called *sambal mateh*. If the relish doesn't appeal or you can't find the ingredients, you can also serve the squash with any of the green sauces on pages 224–27.

NOTE. Fresh or frozen kaffir lime leaves are available at specialty stores and Asian markets. If you can't find them, substitute 2 teaspoons chopped jarred kaffir lime leaves, available at Trader Joe's.

POTLUCK PREP. The squash can be roasted up to 1 day ahead. Bring to room temperature before serving. The relish is best the day it's made, and can stand at room temperature for several hours.

Preheat the oven to 400°F. Line a baking sheet with parchment paper.

Arrange the squash wedges on the prepared baking sheet. If the coconut oil is hard, gently warm it in a microwave or on the stove. Brush the squash all over with 2 tablespoons of the oil and season with salt and pepper. Roast for about 30 minutes, turning once halfway through, until very tender and browned in spots.

Meanwhile, in a bowl, mix the shallot with the lime juice and let stand for 10 minutes.

Cut off the bottom inch and top green part of the lemongrass stalks. Remove the outer three layers so you're left with the tender pieces. Thinly slice crosswise. You should have about ¼ cup.

Add the lemongrass to the shallot along with the lime leaves, fish sauce, and remaining ¼ cup coconut oil. Add 1 thinly sliced chile and let stand for 10 minutes. Taste the relish. If you and your crowd can handle more heat, add more chile until the heat is to your liking. (It will get spicier as it stands.)

Arrange the squash wedges on a platter and garnish with peanuts and scallion greens. Dollop the relish over the squash or serve it alongside.

ON GRILLING AND ROASTING VEGETABLES

Back in the dark ages of vegetable cookery, people overcooked their Brussels sprouts and popped open a can for green beans. Now that we glorify vegetables as much as we do meat, we've learned ways to show off their best attributes. If steaming is how to showcase vegetables at their purest, roasting or grilling is how vegetables are their tastiest. The high, dry heat of the oven or grill caramelizes their natural sugars, adding layers of flavor you never knew were there.

Roasted or grilled vegetables are a great addition to any potluck because you can make them in advance and they are delicious at room temperature. You can also vary the vegetables by season, so you can essentially bring the same dish over and over, but no one will ever know. Plus, vegetables are gorgeous. You can just pile a mixed variety of them on a platter and sprinkle them with herbs or seeds or crumbled cheese. If you're feeling ambitious, drizzle them with a dressing or one of the green sauces on pages 224–27. It's as simple as that.

Here, some general tips for roasting and grilling vegetables, followed by a veggie-by-veggie way to prepare them.

ROASTED VEGGIE RULES

1. If you're roasting multiple types of vegetables together, either cut them so they're all about the same size or roast them on separate parts of the baking sheets so you can pull them off when you need to.

2. To go into a hot, dry oven, most vegetables need protection. Toss them with olive oil, coconut oil, or a neutral oil, and then season well with salt. Bonus: The oil helps the vegetables brown better and the salt brings out their sweet flavors.

3. I like to use a large rimmed baking sheet with shallow sides, and then line it with parchment paper to save on cleanup and prevent sticking. Spread the vegetables out so there's space between each piece and they'll brown nicely.

4. There are mixed views about the optimal oven temperature. I tend toward the 400°F to 450°F range, as they get nicely browned, crisp, and tender before they're charred. But if you prefer a juicier vegetable and a more evenly golden look, here's a tip from City

Bakery in New York City: Roast the veggies at 375°F and put a roasting pan of water on the bottom of the oven. For super-browned and crisp veggies, put the pan in the bottom of the oven (just watch to make sure they don't char). For lighter browning, roast them in the center or top of the oven.

5. Stir or flip the vegetables at least once halfway through so both sides get evenly browned.

GRILLED VEGGIE RULES

1. As with roasting, grilled vegetables require a little oil and salt. It also helps to oil the grates. (I oil a paper towel and use tongs to rub it on.)

2. Much like meat, you can marinate vegetables, to give them even more flavor. Vinaigrettes work particularly well as does, believe it or not, mayonnaise, which blisters beautifully on the grill.

3. Most vegetables grill best over medium-high heat, which is hot enough to char them *and* get them tender. (Firm vegetables might need to be blanched first or cooked through on a cooler part of the grill after they're charred.) If your grill has obvious hot spots, move the vegetables around so they cook evenly.

4. For smaller vegetables that risk falling through the grates, use a perforated grill pan. You can also set an oiled piece of perforated foil over the grates.

5. If grill marks are a priority for you, keep the vegetables in one spot for 2 to 3 minutes before shifting them.

6. Vegetables often grill quickly, so be prepared. Bring tongs for flipping and a baking sheet or large platter to use as a landing spot for just-cooked vegetables.

VEGGIE-BY-VEGGIE TIPS FOR ROASTING OR GRILLING

ASPARAGUS. Roast medium to large spears for about 10 minutes in the oven or grill for about 7 minutes, arranging them perpendicular to the grates.

BEETS. Wrap unpeeled beets in foil, set into a baking dish, and roast until they can be pierced with a fork, 30 minutes to 1 hour or more, depending on their size. Rub off the skins. Or, you can peel them first and cut them into wedges or dice and roast them, covered with foil, for the first half of the cooking. For grilling, peel and blanch first before slicing into slabs and grilling.

BELGIAN ENDIVE, RADICCHIO, AND TREVISO. These bitter veggies become mellow and sweet when grilled or roasted. To prepare, halve or quarter them through the core, and brush with oil.

BROCCOLI, CAULIFLOWER, AND THE LIKE. You can pretty much cut the pieces how you want—sliced so they're tree-like or pulled into large or small florets. When grilling, it's best to blanch them first, and then grill briefly, until just charred.

BRUSSELS SPROUTS. To roast, just halve them or quarter them before oiling and salting. Grill using a perforated pan.

CABBAGE. Cut a head lengthwise through the core to create wedges or slabs. You can pull them out of the oven or grill when they're crisp-tender, for salads, or let them go longer if you prefer.

CARROTS. When roasting, blanch if you're looking for a juicier-seeming carrot, or just put them right in the oven. Baby or other smaller carrots work well; keep them whole or halve them lengthwise. For larger carrots going into the oven, cut them however you please; for the grill, blanch whole carrots first or slice large carrots on the diagonal into slabs that are at least ½ inch thick.

CELERY ROOT. Peel with a sharp knife. To roast, cut into cubes. When grilling, cut into ½-inch-thick slabs, and blanch if you want to speed up the process.

CORN. For either method, pull off the silk and leave on the husks (as I do in the Grilled Corn Salad with Lime Mayo, Cilantro, and Radishes, page 149), which helps keep the kernels juicy. If you like your corn more charred, remove the husks completely and brush with oil.

EGGPLANT. To use eggplant in a puree or dip (like the Red Pepper, Eggplant, and Walnut Dip, page 34), prick it with a fork and roast it, broil it, or even grill it whole over medium heat. Otherwise, you can peel it (optional), cut into slabs or cubes, toss with plenty of oil, and roast. (For the grill, stick with slabs.)

FAVA BEANS. While rarely roasted, fava beans, grilled right in the pods, are spectacular. Toss the pods with seasoning or dressing and serve them for people to peel and eat. The smallest, freshest beans can actually be eaten while they're still in the pods (seriously).

FENNEL. After you remove the stalks, slice the bulb lengthwise into slabs or into wedges. Because fennel bulbs are so firm and can get leathery in the dry heat, cover the wedges with foil for the first half of roasting. When grilling, start over medium-high heat and then move pieces to a cooler part of the grill to cook through.

GARLIC. Toss unpeeled garlic cloves with your roasted vegetable mix or cook the head whole: Cut off the top parts of the head to reveal the cloves, set on 2 sheets of foil, drizzle with oil, and close up the package. Roast or set on a medium-heat grill; the heads will take at least 45 minutes to cook. Spread the soft, sweet cloves on bread or whisk into dressings.

GREEN BEANS AND THE LIKE. Leave beans whole to roast and start checking them after 15 or so minutes. They'll become shriveled and a little blistered but incredibly sweet. On the grill, use a perforated grill pan.

KALE. For crisp kale, you can roast oil- or marinade-coated chopped stemmed leaves at 375°F for about 15 minutes. When grilling, keep the leaves whole (stems and all), toss them with oil, and set them on the grates for a few minutes per side.

MUSHROOMS. Roast mushrooms whole (which will keep them juiciest), in chunks, or sliced. On the grill, you can set the heftier ones right on the grates or skewer the little guys so they don't fall through.

OKRA. Hot dry heat does okra well because it tends to be less slimy when cooked this way. You can leave the pods whole or, to make them even less slimy, halve them lengthwise. Grill on skewers.

ONIONS, LEEKS, AND SCALLIONS. When roasting, halve or quarter the smaller ones and cut the larger ones into wedges. On the grill, lengthwise slabs that are cut through the core work well. For leeks, remove the top dark green parts, halve lengthwise, wash well, and roast or grill. Scallions, which cook in just a few minutes, are best left whole.

PARSNIPS. Cut them into ¾- to 1-inch pieces and roast alone or with other root veggies. If you want to try them grilled, definitely parboil and cut on the diagonal into slabs.

PEPPERS. If you're impatient, like me, roast your peppers over a gas flame or under a broiler until the skin blackens, then transfer to a bowl, cover, and let stand for 10 or so minutes; rub off the skin. Or roast peppers whole at 375°F, turning every 20 minutes or so, until browned and blistered and tender, about 1 hour. Peel both types of peppers when cooled. For the grill, cut the flesh of bell peppers lengthwise off the cores and toss in oil. For smaller peppers or chiles, grill them whole, then stem, seed, and peel later. (Wear gloves if you're dealing with anything that's spicy!)

POTATOES. Roast fingerlings whole or halved lengthwise. Cut larger potatoes into 1-inch pieces or so. For the grill, boil the potatoes whole until they're just tender, and then halve the small ones or cut the larger ones into slabs before tossing with oil and grilling.

RADISHES. As with sugar snap peas, roast radishes at high heat for a short amount of time so they stay crisp-tender. Halve them to get the cut sides nicely browned. For the grill, use a perforated pan and leave the radishes whole.

ROMAINE LETTUCE. To grill or roast, halve romaine lettuce hearts lengthwise, brush with oil, and cook until the tender parts of the leaves are browned or charred and the white parts are crisp-tender. This approach works well for bok choy, too.

SUGAR SNAP PEAS. Keep the peas whole and roast in a super-hot oven (about 475°F) for a few minutes; you want them to brown without losing their crispness. For a grill, use a perforated grill pan and blast them quickly.

SUMMER SQUASH AND ZUCCHINI. When prepping for the oven, cut them into rounds, which cook quickly (about 10 minutes), or larger chunks or sticks, which take about twice the time. For the grill, I like to cook lengthwise slabs that are about ⅓ inch thick.

SUNCHOKES (JERUSALEM ARTICHOKES). The easiest way to roast them is just to scrub them and leave them whole; the flesh becomes incredibly fluffy this way; you can slice or cut into chunks first if you prefer. Blanch and halve before grilling.

SWEET POTATOES. To roast whole, poke them all over with a fork as you would a baked potato or cut into small pieces and toss with other root veggies. For the grill, blanch until just barely tender, cut into slabs or large wedges, and grill just until charred.

TOMATOES. You can roast tomatoes low and slow (as is done in the Fregola with Tuna, Capers, and Slow-Roasted Tomatoes on page 64), so they dry out without coloring, or high and fast, so they become more browned. Just halve plum tomatoes and smaller ones; slice the larger ones into rounds. When grilling, cut larger tomatoes into wedges and peel after you grill, if desired.

TURNIPS AND RUTABAGA. For smaller turnips, it's usually easiest and prettiest to halve them or cut them into wedges. For larger vegetables, chopped into chunks is best. For the grill, go with wedges.

WINTER SQUASH. In general, if you're cooking a squash for a puree, you can just halve it, seed it, and roast it cut side down and then scoop out the flesh. Otherwise, cut the squash into wedges, chunks, or slabs and roast until tender and browned on the outside. While you can serve most varieties of squash skin on, butternut needs to be peeled. For the grill, cut the squash into slabs or wedges and parboil before grilling.

SPICED SLOW-COOKED ROMANO BEANS

VEGAN; GLUTEN-FREE / SERVES 6 TO 10

- 1 LARGE RIPE TOMATO (ABOUT 12 OUNCES), HALVED
- ¼ CUP EXTRA-VIRGIN OLIVE OIL
- 1 MEDIUM YELLOW ONION, FINELY CHOPPED (1½ CUPS)
- 3 GARLIC CLOVES, THINLY SLICED

- KOSHER SALT
- ½ TEASPOON CUMIN SEEDS
- ½ TEASPOON CORIANDER SEEDS
- ¼ TEASPOON CARAWAY SEEDS
- 1 DRIED RED CHILE, SUCH AS CHILE DE ÁRBOL
- 1 TEASPOON TOMATO PASTE

- 1 TEASPOON POMEGRANATE MOLASSES
- 2 POUNDS FLAT ROMANO BEANS, GREEN BEANS, OR A MIXTURE OF THE TWO, TRIMMED AND HALVED CROSSWISE

This is a vegetable dish—but I have to say, it barely tastes like one. (Case in point: when I served it to my then two-year-old daughter, she asked for more noodles.) I like to use flat romano beans when I can find them at the farmers' market because they practically melt, becoming completely infused with the spiced sauce. The bit of pomegranate molasses here is what really sets this dish apart, but if you can't find it, add a little honey and lemon juice to balance the flavors to your liking.

POTLUCK PREP. The cooked beans can be refrigerated for up to 3 days.

Grate the cut sides of the tomato on the coarse holes of a box grater into a bowl or liquid measuring cup until you reach the tomato skin; you should have about 1 cup tomato puree.

In a large, deep skillet with a lid or a wide pot, heat the olive oil over medium heat. Add the onion and garlic, season with salt, and cook until the onion is very soft, about 10 minutes. Add the cumin, coriander, caraway seeds, and the chile, and cook until fragrant, about 1 minute. Add the tomato paste and cook until it starts to coat the bottom of the pan and darkens, 1 to 2 minutes. Add the tomato puree, the pomegranate molasses, and beans and stir to coat.

Bring the liquid to a boil, reduce the heat to medium-low, cover, and simmer gently, stirring occasionally, until very tender and infused with the sauce, 45 minutes to 1 hour depending on the toughness of your beans. The tomato should provide enough liquid for the beans to cook, but if you're afraid the bottom of your pan might scorch, add a couple of tablespoons of water.

Uncover and simmer the sauce until thickened as desired, less than 10 minutes. Season with more salt, then serve warm, at room temperature, or even chilled.

ROASTED AND RAW BRUSSELS SPROUTS SALAD
WITH PECORINO AND POMEGRANATE

VEGETARIAN; GLUTEN-FREE / SERVES 6 TO 12

2 POUNDS BRUSSELS SPROUTS

½ CUP EXTRA-VIRGIN OLIVE OIL

KOSHER SALT AND FRESHLY GROUND BLACK PEPPER

1 (2-OUNCE) CHUNK PECORINO-ROMANO CHEESE

ARILS FROM 1 POME-GRANATE (ABOUT ¾ CUP; SEE NOTE), OR 1 MEDIUM GRANNY SMITH OR HONEY CRISP APPLE, CORED AND FINELY CHOPPED

3 TABLESPOONS FRESH LEMON JUICE, PLUS MORE FOR SEASONING

¼ CUP CHOPPED FRESH FLAT-LEAF PARSLEY

This satisfying salad shows off two great ways to use Brussels sprouts: as caramelized, roasted chunks and as sweet, raw shreds. To turn this into an even heftier salad, add some cooked lentils or grains, like barley or faro.

NOTE. To remove the arils from a pomegranate, use a sharp knife to halve it crosswise. Fill a bowl with cold water. Hold one of the pomegranate halves with the seeds side down over the bowl and whack it hard all over with a wooden spoon, until most of the seeds fall into the bowl. Repeat with the other pomegranate half. Skim off the white pith and drain the seeds.

POTLUCK PREP. The salad can be refrigerated overnight. Bring to a cool room temperature and taste and re-season, if necessary, before serving. It can stand at room temperature for 2 hours.

Preheat the oven to 425°F. Line a large, rimmed baking sheet with parchment paper.

Trim and quarter, lengthwise, about three-fourths of the Brussels sprouts. Put the sprouts in a large bowl, toss them with 3 tablespoons of the olive oil, and season with salt and pepper. Spread them out on the prepared baking sheet and roast for about 30 minutes, until browned and tender. Let cool to warm.

Halve and thinly slice, crosswise, the remaining one-fourth of the Brussels sprouts so they're shredded. Put them into a large bowl and add the roasted sprouts.

Using a vegetable peeler, shave the cheese and break it into rough pieces. (You should have a heaping ½ cup.) Add the cheese to the bowl of sprouts and toss with the pomegranate arils, lemon juice, and the remaining 5 tablespoons olive oil. Season with salt and pepper and more lemon juice, if desired. Add the parsley, toss again, and serve.

VEGETARIAN BORSCHT SALAD

VEGETARIAN; GLUTEN-FREE / SERVES 6 TO 12

1½ POUNDS CARROTS (8 TO 10 MEDIUM), SCRUBBED AND CUT INTO 2-INCH CHUNKS

3 TABLESPOONS EXTRA-VIRGIN OLIVE OIL

KOSHER SALT AND FRESHLY GROUND BLACK PEPPER

2 MEDIUM ONIONS, EACH CUT INTO 10 WEDGES

1½ POUNDS BEETS (ABOUT 4 LARGE), PEELED AND EACH CUT INTO 8 WEDGES

4 TEASPOONS RED WINE OR SHERRY VINEGAR

¼ CUP ROUGHLY CHOPPED FRESH DILL, PLUS MORE FOR GARNISH

SOUR CREAM, FOR SERVING

I love borscht, so I took some of the vegetables in the vibrant, flavorful soup—including beets, carrots, and onion—and turned them into a roasted vegetable salad, dressed with plenty of vinegar and dill. To make the salad extra stunning, use mixed colors of carrots and beets.

POTLUCK PREP. The dressed roasted vegetables without the dill can be refrigerated overnight. (If you prefer that the colors not bleed, separate them by color before you toss them with the vinegar.) Add the sour cream and dill soon before serving.

Preheat the oven to 425°F. Line 2 baking sheets with parchment paper or foil.

In a large bowl, toss the carrots with 1 tablespoon of the olive oil and season with salt and pepper. Arrange the carrots in one section of one of the prepared baking sheets. Repeat with the onions, followed by the beet wedges, arranging each of the vegetables in its own section of the baking sheets. Cover the baking sheets with foil.

Roast for about 20 minutes, until the vegetables are nearly tender. Remove the foil and rotate the baking sheets. Roast for 10 to 20 minutes longer, until the vegetables are nicely tender and browned in spots. Let cool to warm.

Return the vegetables to the bowl and toss with the vinegar. Let stand for 5 minutes. Add the ¼ cup dill and toss again. Spread the salad out on a platter. Dollop sour cream on top, garnish with more dill, and serve.

SLOW-COOKED SMOKY AND SAVORY GREENS

VEGAN; GLUTEN-FREE / SERVES 6 TO 10

3 POUNDS CHARD, KALE
(ANY TYPE), OR COLLARD
GREENS (SEE NOTE)

¼ CUP PLUS 2 TABLESPOONS
EXTRA-VIRGIN OLIVE OIL

6 OUNCES SHALLOTS, THINLY
SLICED (ABOUT 1½ CUPS)

KOSHER SALT AND
FRESHLY GROUND
BLACK PEPPER

6 GARLIC CLOVES, MINCED
OR GRATED

¼ CUP TOMATO PASTE

1 TEASPOON SMOKED
PAPRIKA

½ CUP WATER

Long before the ubiquitous kale salad, greens were cooked low and slow until they were so tender they practically melted. In the American South and in Italy, greens are often cooked with a little cured pork. Here, I add tomato paste and smoked paprika instead, which give them a deep savory flavor so they taste almost meaty. Some cooks absolutely hate including the stems in their cooked greens. I don't really mind them when the greens are on the tender side, but the choice is yours.

Cut off and discard the bottom 1 inch of stem from the greens. Strip the stems from the leaves. If you plan to cook the stems, slice them crosswise ½ inch thick, keeping them separate from the leaves. Coarsely chop the leaves. At this point, I like to wash the greens and leave them wet so any remaining moisture helps them wilt.

In a large, deep skillet or a large pot, heat the olive oil over medium-high heat. Add the shallots, season with salt and pepper, and cook, stirring, until they're just starting to brown, 3 to 4 minutes. Stir in the garlic and cook until fragrant, about 1 minute. Stir in the tomato paste and cook until it starts to coat the bottom of the pan and darken, 1 to 2 minutes. Add the paprika and cook for about 30 seconds. Stir in the chopped stems, if using, and then add the water. Reduce the heat to medium, cover, and steam until bright green and just starting to soften, about 3 minutes.

Add large handfuls of greens to the pan, stirring and waiting for them to wilt down before adding more. Add the water to the pan if you haven't already, cover, and braise over medium heat, stirring every 5 minutes or so to prevent the tomato paste from scorching, for at least 15 minutes. At this point, the Swiss chard should be tender; the kale or collards will likely be tender with some chew. For super-silky greens, keep cooking them, tasting as you go and adding more water as necessary. You can cook them for as long as 1 hour or even more if they're especially tough; they're done when you say so. Season with salt and pepper, and serve.

NOTE. Three pounds of greens is a lot to prep and does take time. To stem the greens, either hold them by the stem and use your thumb and forefinger to slide the leaves off the stalks or else slice them out of the leaves using a knife, making an upside-down V-shape in the leaves.

POTLUCK PREP. The cooked greens can be refrigerated overnight and are great hot or at room temperature. If you like them hot, consider serving them from a slow cooker, being sure you have a little liquid (also known as potlikker) in the cooker. For room-temperature greens, transfer them to a serving dish using a slotted spoon, leaving the potlikker behind; then reduce the liquid so only a little remains, pour it over the greens, and serve.

BAKED & SAVORY

ASPARAGUS QUICHE
WITH RYE CRUST

VEGETARIAN / MAKES ONE 9-INCH QUICHE

FOR THE PASTRY

1 TABLESPOON CIDER VINEGAR

½ CUP ICE WATER

1 CUP ALL-PURPOSE FLOUR

¾ CUP WHOLE-GRAIN (DARK) RYE FLOUR

1 TEASPOON KOSHER SALT

½ TEASPOON GROUND CARAWAY (OPTIONAL)

½ CUP (1 STICK) UNSALTED BUTTER, COLD, CUBED

FOR THE FILLING

1 TABLESPOON BUTTER

10 RAMPS, TRIMMED AND THINLY SLICED, OR 8 SCALLIONS, WHITE AND LIGHT GREEN PARTS CUT INTO ¾-INCH PIECES AND DARK GREEN PARTS THINLY SLICED

¾ POUND ASPARAGUS, TRIMMED AND SLICED INTO 1-INCH LENGTHS

KOSHER SALT AND FRESHLY GROUND WHITE PEPPER

3 LARGE EGGS

1 CUP HALF-AND-HALF

1 CUP SHREDDED GRUYÈRE CHEESE (4 OUNCES)

Quiche is incredibly old-fashioned, but when it's made well—with a custardy filling and a crisp, flaky crust—it's a luxurious treat. This vegetable-heavy quiche has just enough custard to hold it together. Feel free to mix up the filling: you can substitute 2 cups of cooked vegetables or meat for the asparagus and ramps or switch up the cheese.

The rye flour in the pastry gives the quiche an appealing rustic flavor that's especially nice in spring. You can substitute all-purpose flour or whole-wheat, if you prefer.

MAKE THE PASTRY: In a liquid measuring cup, combine the vinegar with the ice water.

In a large bowl, whisk the flours with the salt and caraway. Add the butter and, using a pastry blender or your fingers, mix until most of the butter is the size of peas with a few larger chunks remaining. (You can also do this in a food processor.)

Mix in the vinegar mixture, tablespoon by tablespoon, until the dough just starts to hold together with a few dry spots remaining (this will happen somewhere between 6 and 8 tablespoons). Turn the dough out onto a work surface. Lightly knead any ragged edges and form the dough into a ball. Flatten the ball into a disk, wrap in plastic, and refrigerate for at least 2 hours.

On a lightly floured work surface, roll out the pastry to a 13-inch round that's a scant ¼ inch thick. Because of the rye flour, the dough may crack a bit; if it does, use outer scraps to patch any holes or cracks.

(RECIPE CONTINUES)

Fit the dough into a 9-inch glass pie plate and trim the overhang to ¾ inch. Fold the dough edge under itself and crimp; use the scraps to patch any tiny cracks or holes (this is important because the filling is liquid and will seep out). Refrigerate for at least 10 minutes.

Preheat the oven to 350°F.

Line the shell with parchment paper or foil and fill with beans, rice, or pie weights. Bake for 20 minutes and then remove the weights and parchment. Bake for 10 to 15 more minutes, until the crust is just starting to brown. Let cool completely.

MEANWHILE, PREPARE THE FILLING: In a skillet, melt the butter over medium-high heat. Add the white and light green parts of the ramps and all of the asparagus, season lightly with salt and pepper, and cook until the asparagus is crisp-tender, 4 to 6 minutes. Add the dark green parts of the ramps and cook until wilted, about 20 seconds. Let cool.

In a large bowl, whisk the eggs with the half-and-half and ½ teaspoon each salt and white pepper.

Set the pie plate with the crust on a rimmed baking sheet. Sprinkle the bottom of the crust with the cheese; top with the asparagus mixture. Pour the egg mixture over the filling until you just reach the bottom rim of the crust; you may have a couple of tablespoons of liquid left over.

Bake, rotating the sheet halfway through, until the center is just set, about 45 minutes. Let the quiche stand for at least 15 minutes before serving. Serve warm or at room temperature.

POTLUCK PREP. The pastry dough can be refrigerated for up to 3 days and frozen for up to 1 month; thaw in the refrigerator. The baked quiche can be refrigerated for up to 2 days. Cover and reheat at 325°F for 15 to 20 minutes.

WHITE WHOLE WHEAT PUMPKIN BISCUITS

VEGETARIAN / MAKES ABOUT 14 BISCUITS

2¼ CUPS WHITE WHOLE WHEAT FLOUR, PLUS MORE FOR DUSTING

1 TABLESPOON BAKING POWDER

1 TEASPOON KOSHER SALT

2 TABLESPOONS MAPLE SUGAR OR LIGHT BROWN SUGAR

½ CUP (1 STICK) UNSALTED BUTTER, COLD, CUT INTO CUBES, PLUS 1 TABLESPOON MELTED BUTTER, FOR BRUSHING

1 CUP CHILLED PUMPKIN PUREE

¾ CUP CHILLED BUTTERMILK

FLAKY SALT, FOR SPRINKLING

Oakland, California, chef Tanya Holland created a delicious sweet potato biscuit for a Thanksgiving story I worked on while at *Food & Wine*. These biscuits are based on hers, but I use healthier white whole wheat flour instead of all-purpose. For ease, I call for canned pumpkin puree, but you can also use mashed sweet potatoes or pureed butternut squash instead.

VARIATIONS

SAVORY SPICED BISCUITS. Reduce the sugar to 1 tablespoon. Add ¼ teaspoon each ground cumin, coriander, and cinnamon, and ⅛ teaspoon smoked paprika to the dry ingredients for biscuits that are great with chili.

SWEET SPICED BISCUITS. Add 1 more tablespoon of sugar, along with ½ teaspoon ground cinnamon and ¼ teaspoon nutmeg. Sprinkle with turbinado sugar and serve with roasted apples or pears.

Preheat the oven to 450°F. Line a baking sheet with parchment paper.

In a large bowl, whisk the flour with the baking powder, salt, and maple sugar. Sprinkle the cubed butter over the dry ingredients and use a pastry blender or your fingers to work in the butter until it looks like coarse crumbs with some pieces that are about the size of peas.

In a small bowl, whisk the pumpkin puree with the buttermilk. Stir the mixture into the dry ingredients just until a soft dough forms. Turn the dough out onto a floured work surface and pat it into a 1-inch-thick round. Using a 2-inch round biscuit cutter, stamp out as many biscuits as you can. Gently press the scraps together and stamp out more biscuits. (Alternatively, you can press the dough into a square and cut out square biscuits.) Arrange the biscuits on the prepared baking sheet, brush with butter, and sprinkle with flaky salt.

Bake for 12 to 15 minutes, until golden brown. Serve warm or at room temperature.

POTLUCK PREP. The biscuits are best the day they are made. To transport while hot, wrap in a clean towel or cloth napkin.

CARAMELIZED ONION, GOUDA, AND PECAN SCONES

VEGETARIAN / MAKES 8 LARGE SCONES OR 32 MINI SCONES

½ CUP (1 STICK) UNSALTED BUTTER, 1 TABLESPOON LEFT WHOLE, 7 TABLESPOONS CUT INTO ½-INCH PIECES AND CHILLED

1 MEDIUM ONION, THINLY SLICED (ABOUT 1 CUP)

1 CUP ALL-PURPOSE FLOUR

1 CUP WHOLE WHEAT FLOUR

2 TEASPOONS SUGAR

1½ TEASPOONS BAKING POWDER

½ TEASPOON BAKING SODA

½ TEASPOON KOSHER SALT

4 OUNCES YOUNG GOUDA CHEESE (RED WAX GOUDA IS FINE) OR SMOKED GOUDA, COARSELY GRATED (1 HEAPING CUP)

½ CUP PECANS, ROUGHLY CHOPPED (ABOUT 2 OUNCES)

¾ CUP BUTTERMILK

These hefty savory scones are almost like a meal unto themselves. They're great on a brunch table or served with ham for sandwiches or passed as a side at a soup party. You can also make mini scones for a cocktail party because they're absolutely fantastic with Champagne. If you'd like a hint of heat, add a small pinch of cayenne with the dry ingredients. And if you don't want to wait for the onion to caramelize, add 2 thinly sliced raw scallions instead.

In a medium skillet set over medium heat, melt the whole tablespoon of butter. Add the onion and cook, stirring occasionally, until soft, about 8 minutes. Increase the heat to medium-high; as some of the onion browns and seems like it might burn, add a teaspoon or so of water. Continue cooking, stirring and adding a little water as necessary, until the onion is very soft and very browned, about 10 more minutes. Make sure all of the liquid has evaporated, then scrape into a bowl and refrigerate to cool.

Grease a large baking sheet or line it with parchment paper or a Silpat liner.

In a large bowl, whisk the flours with the sugar, baking powder, baking soda, and salt. Add the remaining 7 tablespoons butter and use a pastry blender or your fingers to mix it in until it looks like coarse crumbs with some pieces that are about the size of peas. Add the cheese and pecans and use a wooden spoon or your hands to toss until combined.

Add the buttermilk and the onion and stir just until incorporated. Use your hands to lightly knead the mixture until it holds together; the less you handle it, the more tender the scones will be.

Turn the dough out onto a lightly floured surface and gently pat into an 8½-inch round that's about ½ inch thick. Use a sharp knife to cut the round into 8 wedges. Arrange the wedges close together on the prepared baking sheet and refrigerate for about 30 minutes.

Preheat the oven to 375°F.

Bake, turning the baking sheet once halfway through, for about 20 minutes, until golden. Transfer the scones to a wire rack and let cool to warm or room temperature. Serve.

VARIATION. To make mini scones, pat the dough into an 8-inch square. Cut the square into sixteen 2-inch squares, and then halve each square on the diagonal to form a mini wedge. Bake as directed, checking them for doneness after 10 minutes.

POTLUCK PREP. The scones are best the day they're made. To transport warm scones, wrap in a clean towel or cloth napkin.

CLOTILDE'S FRENCH QUICK BREAD
WITH PEARS, WALNUTS, AND ROQUEFORT

VEGETARIAN / MAKES ONE 9 × 5-INCH LOAF CAKE

¼ CUP EXTRA-VIRGIN OLIVE OIL, PLUS MORE FOR THE PAN

1¼ CUPS ALL-PURPOSE FLOUR

1 TABLESPOON BAKING POWDER

3 LARGE EGGS

½ TEASPOON FINE SEA SALT

½ TEASPOON FRESHLY GROUND BLACK PEPPER

½ CUP PLAIN WHOLE-MILK GREEK-STYLE YOGURT

3½ OUNCES ROQUEFORT CHEESE (OR THE BLUE CHEESE OF YOUR CHOICE), CRUMBLED

1 RIPE BOSC PEAR, CORED AND CHOPPED

½ CUP WALNUTS, ROUGHLY CHOPPED (ABOUT 2 OUNCES)

Clotilde Dusoulier, author of the books *The French Market Cookbook* and *Edible French,* and the blog *Chocolate and Zucchini,* started blogging about the time I was going to culinary school. I've loved watching her transform from amateur cook to professional food writer, and I was thrilled when she agreed to contribute this recipe. She says:

"Although the French don't officially do potlucks, there are plenty of occasions for buffet-style meals. If there is one item you can be certain of finding in such edible spreads, it is the *cake salé,* or savory loaf, a quick bread that is sliced or cubed, and very easy to eat while talking and balancing a glass of wine. This version is a fall and winter favorite, featuring the classic French trio of pear, walnuts, and blue cheese. I like to use Roquefort, but feel free to substitute the blue cheese you prefer."

Preheat the oven to 350° F. Generously coat a 9 × 5-inch loaf pan with olive oil.

In a small bowl, sift together the flour and baking powder; set aside.

In a medium bowl, beat the eggs, salt, and pepper until pale and frothy. Whisk in the ¼ cup olive oil and the yogurt. Fold in the dry ingredients until no trace of flour remains, but don't overmix; the batter should be a bit lumpy. Fold in the cheese, pear, and walnuts. Pour the batter into the prepared pan and smooth the surface with a spatula.

Bake for 40 to 50 minutes, until the top of the loaf is golden and a knife inserted in the center comes out clean. Let cool for a few minutes. Run a knife around the edges of the pan to loosen, unmold, and transfer to a wire rack to cool. Serve at room temperature, sliced or cubed.

POTLUCK PREP. The cake can stand at room temperature overnight.

CARAMELIZED KIMCHI CORN BREAD

VEGETARIAN (OPTIONAL) / MAKES ONE 9 × 13-INCH CORN BREAD

- ½ CUP (1 STICK) UNSALTED BUTTER, MELTED, PLUS MORE FOR THE PAN
- 3 CUPS WELL-DRAINED CABBAGE KIMCHI (ABOUT 1½ POUNDS) (USE VEGETARIAN KIMCHI, IF NECESSARY)
- ½ CUP CIDER VINEGAR
- ¼ CUP PLUS 2 TABLESPOONS SUGAR
- 2 CUPS ALL-PURPOSE FLOUR
- 2 CUPS STONE-GROUND CORNMEAL (MEDIUM GRIND)
- 1 TABLESPOON BAKING POWDER
- ¼ TEASPOON BAKING SODA
- 1 TEASPOON KOSHER SALT
- 2 LARGE EGGS
- 1½ CUPS MILK

Several years ago, chefs starting adding kimchi to everything—and for good reason: the spicy, garlicky Korean pickle adds tons of flavor to anything it touches. I don't know where I got the idea to add kimchi to corn bread, but I'm telling you, the combination is meant to be. The bread tastes like nacho-flavored Doritos—in the best way. After you try this, you might never make plain old corn bread again. (See photograph on pages 170–171.)

POTLUCK PREP. The corn bread is best the day it is made, but can be wrapped in foil and kept at room temperature for up to 2 days. Rewarm slightly to refresh.

Preheat the oven to 350°F. Butter a 9 × 13-inch baking pan, preferably metal.

In a food processor, pulse the kimchi until finely chopped. Transfer to a medium saucepan and add the vinegar and ¼ cup sugar. Cook over medium-high heat, stirring frequently, until the sugar dissolves and the liquid has evaporated, 12 to 15 minutes. Reduce the heat to medium and cook until the kimchi is slightly darker, about 5 more minutes. Let cool.

In a large bowl, whisk the flour with the cornmeal, baking powder, baking soda, and salt.

In a medium bowl, whisk the eggs with the remaining 2 tablespoons sugar and the milk. Add the liquid to the dry ingredients and stir until combined. Stir in the melted butter, and then fold in the kimchi. Pour the batter into the prepared pan.

Bake in the center of the oven for about 30 minutes, until golden and a toothpick inserted in the center comes out clean. Let cool for at least 15 minutes before serving.

MOLLY'S SCALLION PULL-APART BREAD

VEGETARIAN / MAKES ONE 8-INCH ROUND BREAD

FOR THE DOUGH

2¼ TEASPOONS ACTIVE DRY YEAST (1 ENVELOPE)

1 TABLESPOON SUGAR

¾ CUP WARM WATER

3 CUPS ALL-PURPOSE FLOUR, PLUS MORE FOR DUSTING

2 TEASPOONS KOSHER SALT

½ CUP VEGETABLE OR CANOLA OIL, PLUS MORE FOR THE BOWL

FOR THE FILLING

ROASTED SESAME OIL, FOR BRUSHING (ABOUT ¼ CUP)

8 SCALLIONS, FINELY CHOPPED (ABOUT 1 CUP)

KOSHER SALT AND FRESHLY GROUND BLACK PEPPER

RED PEPPER FLAKES

1 LARGE EGG, LIGHTLY BEATEN WITH 1 TABLESPOON WATER, FOR BRUSHING

TOASTED SESAME SEEDS, FOR TOPPING

Molly Yeh is the exuberant voice behind the blog *My Name is Yeh*. After growing up in Minnesota and attending college at Juilliard in New York City, she moved to North Dakota to live with her farmer husband. With her quirky taste in baked goods and her current Midwestern life, I thought she'd come up with something very fitting for a modern potluck. And she did. She says:

"When I got kicked off of the math team in 11th grade, I figured the next best way to pay homage to my Chinese heritage would be to eat a bunch of Chinese food and cook it for all of my friends. If I had to name one dish that has consistently been a hit among my friends, it'd

be scallion pancakes. They're best when they're right out of the pan, so here's a solution that's more potluck friendly: a scallion pancake–inspired pull-apart bread. This impressive loaf will look good even after it's been wrapped up and tossed in the back of your car/bag/bicycle basket, and its pull-apart nature will eliminate your need for a bread knife."

POTLUCK PREP. You can cover the kneaded dough and refrigerate overnight; bring it to room temperature before rolling it out. The baked rolls are best the day they're made, but can be covered in foil and held at room temperature. Rewarm at 325°F.

(RECIPE CONTINUES)

MAKE THE DOUGH: In a glass measuring cup, combine the yeast, sugar, and warm water. Let stand until it foams at the top, about 5 minutes.

Meanwhile, combine the flour and salt in a large bowl or the bowl of a stand mixer fitted with a dough hook. Stir in the yeast mixture and the oil and mix to combine. Knead for 7 to 10 minutes, until smooth and springy. Transfer the dough to a lightly greased bowl, cover with a damp towel or plastic wrap, and let rise until doubled in size, about 2 hours.

MAKE THE FILLING: Brush an 8-inch round cake pan with a thin layer of sesame oil.

On a lightly floured work surface, roll the dough out into a long rectangle that's about 24 inches by 9 inches. Brush the dough with a thin layer of sesame oil, and sprinkle with the scallions, a pinch of salt, a few grinds of pepper, and a pinch or two of red pepper flakes. Roll the long side of the dough up like a jelly roll and brush the outside with more sesame oil. Cut the roll into 1½- to 2-inch pieces and arrange the pieces cut side up in the cake pan. Cover and let it rise for 30 more minutes.

Preheat the oven to 375°F.

Brush the dough with the egg wash and sprinkle with sesame seeds and a bit more salt. Bake for 30 to 35 minutes, until the top begins to brown. Let cool briefly and serve.

JUSTIN'S SWISS CHARD SLAB PIE
WITH SALT AND PEPPER CRUST

VEGETARIAN / MAKES ONE 12 × 16-INCH PIE

FOR THE DOUGH

- 3 CUPS ALL-PURPOSE FLOUR
- 1 TEASPOON KOSHER SALT
- ½ TEASPOON FRESHLY GROUND BLACK PEPPER
- 1¼ CUPS (2½ STICKS) UNSALTED BUTTER, COLD, CUBED
- ⅔ CUP ICE WATER

FOR THE FILLING

- ⅓ CUP EXTRA-VIRGIN OLIVE OIL
- 1 LARGE RED ONION, FINELY CHOPPED
- 4 GARLIC CLOVES, THINLY SLICED
- KOSHER SALT
- 1 TABLESPOON GROUND CORIANDER
- 1 TABLESPOON GROUND GINGER
- RED PEPPER FLAKES
- 3 POUNDS RED SWISS CHARD, STEMS SEPARATED AND CUT INTO ½-INCH PIECES; LEAVES ROUGHLY CHOPPED
- ½ CUP DRY WHITE WINE
- ¾ CUP SOUR CREAM
- FRESHLY GROUND BLACK PEPPER
- 1 LARGE EGG, LIGHTLY BEATEN WITH 1 TABLESPOON WATER, FOR BRUSHING

It's hard to believe that Justin Chapple was once my intern. Thanks to his incredible cooking talent and irresistible personality, he's now a recipe developer for *Food & Wine*, as well as a web video star. Justin splits his time between New York City and his house in the Catskills, where he regularly goes to potlucks. He says:

"Slab pies are a fun way to serve a crowd for dessert. I wanted to create a savory version, so I came up with a filling that's packed with Swiss chard and laced with sour cream for a subtle lusciousness. I make it early in the day, and then carry it to the party right on the baking sheet. That way the host can serve it as is or warm it slightly in the oven."

MAKE THE DOUGH: In a food processor, pulse the flour with the salt and pepper. Add the butter and pulse until the mixture resembles coarse meal with some pea-size pieces remaining. Sprinkle the ice water on top and pulse until the dough just comes together. Scrape the dough out onto a work surface and gather it into a ball; divide in half and pat each half into a 6-inch square. Wrap the squares in plastic and refrigerate until well chilled, about 1 hour.

MEANWHILE, MAKE THE FILLING: In a pot, heat the olive oil over medium-high heat. Add the onion, garlic, and a generous pinch of salt and cook, stirring occasionally, until just softened, about 5 minutes. Add the coriander, ginger, and a pinch of red pepper flakes and cook, stirring, until fragrant, about 30 seconds. Add the chard stems and cook, stirring occasionally, until just softened, about 6 minutes. Stir in the chard leaves in large handfuls, letting them wilt slightly before

(RECIPE CONTINUES)

adding more. Add the wine, reduce the heat to medium, and cook, stirring occasionally, until the leaves are tender and the liquid has evaporated, 10 to 20 minutes. Transfer the mixture to a colander and let cool completely.

Preheat the oven to 400°F. Line a large rimmed baking sheet with parchment paper.

In a large bowl, mix the cooled chard with the sour cream and season with salt, pepper, and more red pepper flakes, if desired.

On a lightly floured work surface, roll out 1 piece of the dough to a 12 × 16-inch rectangle. Slide the dough onto the prepared baking sheet. Spread the filling evenly over the dough, leaving a 1-inch border. Roll out the remaining dough to a 12 × 16-inch rectangle. Ease the dough over the filling, fold the rim over itself, and pinch the edges or crimp decoratively to seal. Cut a few slits in the top of the pie. Brush the egg wash over the top of the pie, and sprinkle lightly with salt and pepper.

Bake for 50 to 55 minutes, until the crust is golden. Let cool for at least 15 minutes before cutting it into squares. Serve warm or at room temperature.

POTLUCK PREP. The chard filling and dough can be refrigerated separately overnight. The pie can also be baked early in the day and served at room temperature.

SPICED CARROT AND GOAT CHEESE STRUDEL

VEGETARIAN / MAKES TWO 14-INCH STRUDELS

4 MEDIUM CARROTS (ABOUT 8 OUNCES TOTAL)

¾ CUP PLUS 2 TABLESPOONS EXTRA-VIRGIN OLIVE OIL

2 GARLIC CLOVES, MINCED

¼ TEASPOON MUSTARD SEEDS

¼ TEASPOON CUMIN SEEDS

KOSHER SALT AND FRESHLY GROUND BLACK PEPPER

PINCH OF RED PEPPER FLAKES (OPTIONAL)

1 (11-OUNCE) LOG FRESH GOAT CHEESE, SOFTENED AT ROOM TEMPERATURE

½ TEASPOON FRESH THYME LEAVES, OR ¼ TEASPOON DRIED

8 SHEETS THAWED PHYLLO DOUGH (FROM 1 FROZEN PACKAGE), PLUS MORE IN CASE OF TEARING

BLACK SESAME SEEDS OR NIGELLA SEEDS

Phyllo dough feels a little old-fashioned, but it's super-easy to work with and creates such spectacularly crisp, flaky layers. Here, the paper-thin sheets get wrapped around cumin-spiced carrots and tangy goat cheese to make a strudel that tastes vaguely Middle Eastern. If you prefer, you can replace the carrots with 2 cups of well-drained cooked greens or mushrooms.

Preheat the oven to 375°F. Line a baking sheet with parchment paper.

Using the coarse shredding blade on a food processor, shred the carrots (alternatively, you can use 2 cups store-bought shredded carrots).

In a large skillet, heat 2 tablespoons of the olive oil over medium heat. Add the garlic, mustard seeds, and cumin seeds and cook, stirring, until fragrant, about 1 minute. Add the carrots and cook, stirring, until just tender, about 3 minutes. Season with salt and pepper and add the red pepper flakes, if desired.

In a bowl, mix the goat cheese with the thyme.

Put the remaining ¾ cup olive oil in a bowl; cover your 8 sheets of phyllo dough with a clean towel to keep them from drying out.

Set one of the sheets of phyllo on a clean surface with one of the longer edges toward you. Generously brush with oil. Top with 3 more sheets of phyllo, brushing each layer with more oil. Spread half the goat cheese in a strip about ½ inch from the bottom edge of the phyllo stack, leaving about 1 inch on either side. Spread half the carrot filling alongside. Roll the phyllo so that the goat cheese is on top of the carrot filling, then roll into a cylinder, tucking in the edges as you go. Transfer the strudel to the prepared baking sheet, brush with more oil, and sprinkle with sesame seeds. Repeat with the remaining ingredients to make a second strudel.

Bake for about 30 minutes, turning the baking sheet halfway through, until golden and crisp. Let cool for at least 10 minutes before serving.

POTLUCK PREP. The strudels are best the day they're made and can stand at room temperature for several hours. You can also refrigerate them overnight and bake at 325°F to refresh.

SWEETS

STRAWBERRY JAM CHEESECAKE BARS
WITH BUCKWHEAT-ALMOND CRUST

GLUTEN-FREE / MAKES ONE 9 × 13-INCH PAN OF BARS

FOR THE CRUST

- ½ CUP (1 STICK) BUTTER, SOFTENED, PLUS MORE FOR THE PAN
- 1 CUP BUCKWHEAT FLOUR
- ¾ CUP ALMOND MEAL
- ½ CUP PACKED LIGHT BROWN SUGAR
- PINCH OF KOSHER SALT

FOR THE FILLING

- 1 (8-OUNCE) PACKAGE CREAM CHEESE
- 1 TUBE (ABOUT 11 OUNCES) FRESH GOAT CHEESE
- ⅔ CUP GRANULATED SUGAR
- 2 LARGE EGGS
- FINELY GRATED ZEST FROM 1 MEDIUM LEMON
- 1½ CUPS QUICKEST STRAWBERRY JAM (PAGE 230) OR STORE-BOUGHT JAM

With goat cheese and lemon zest in the filling, and earthy buckwheat in the crust, this is a grown-up version of cheesecake. I especially love this made with the not-too-sweet Quickest Strawberry Jam (page 230), but any jam works well.

POTLUCK PREP. The unsliced cheesecake bar can be refrigerated in the pan for up to 4 days. Sliced bars can be individually wrapped and refrigerated for up to 3 days.

Preheat the oven to 350°F. Line a 9 × 13-inch pan with parchment paper so the edge overhangs by 1 inch on the long sides. Butter the exposed sides of the pan.

PREPARE THE CRUST: In a large bowl, whisk the buckwheat flour with the almond meal, brown sugar, and salt. Using a pastry blender or your fingers, work the ½ cup of butter into the dry mixture until incorporated. Press the crust into the prepared pan in an even layer.

Bake for about 20 minutes, until dry to the touch. Let cool slightly.

MEANWHILE, MAKE THE FILLING: In a large bowl, using a handheld electric mixer, beat the cream cheese with the goat cheese, sugar, eggs, and lemon zest until fluffy. Spread the filling over the warm crust.

Bake for 15 minutes, until the top feels dry. Spread the jam over the cheese filling and bake for 10 to 15 more minutes, until sticky. Transfer the pan to a wire rack and let cool completely. Refrigerate for at least 3 hours, until well chilled.

Use the paper to lift the cheesecake out of the pan, slice into bars, and serve.

LEMON-BERRY BUNDT CAKE
WITH RICOTTA AND CORNMEAL

VEGETARIAN / MAKES 1 BUNDT CAKE

FOR THE CAKE

- ¾ CUP (1½ STICKS) UNSALTED BUTTER, SOFTENED, PLUS MORE FOR THE PAN
- 2 CUPS ALL-PURPOSE FLOUR, PLUS MORE FOR DUSTING
- 1 CUP CORNMEAL
- 1½ TEASPOONS BAKING POWDER
- ½ TEASPOON BAKING SODA
- 1 TEASPOON KOSHER SALT

- ZEST OF 2 LEMONS
- 2 CUPS SUGAR
- 1½ CUPS RICOTTA
- 3 LARGE EGGS
- ¼ CUP FRESH LEMON JUICE
- 3 CUPS MIXED LATE-SUMMER BERRIES, SUCH AS BLUEBERRIES, RASPBERRIES, AND BLACKBERRIES, THAWED IF FROZEN

FOR THE GLAZE

- ¼ CUP MIXED LATE-SUMMER BERRIES, THAWED IF FROZEN
- ¼ CUP WATER
- 1 CUP CONFECTIONERS' SUGAR

Lauren Chattman's lovely little book, *Cake Keeper's Cakes*, is one I turn to regularly when I'm looking for something simple to bake. It was a recipe in her book that inspired me to add ricotta to this mixed-berry Bundt cake, which, as she says, creates a lighter crumb.

The pink glaze made with berry juice is stunning. If you'd prefer to have a white glaze, substitute fresh lemon juice.

Preheat the oven to 325°F. Generously butter and flour every crevice of a Bundt pan or spray with a baking spray that contains flour. Line a baking sheet with parchment paper and set a rack on top to use for cooling.

MAKE THE CAKE: In a medium bowl, whisk the flour with the cornmeal, baking powder, baking soda, and salt.

In a large bowl, rub the lemon zest with the sugar until the sugar is slightly moistened. Using an electric mixer, beat the sugar with the ¾ cup butter at medium speed until fluffy, about 3 minutes. Add the ricotta and beat until incorporated. Add the eggs, one at a time, beating until incorporated. Add the lemon juice. Add the dry ingredients in 3 additions, beating well between each addition. Very gently fold in the berries. Scrape the batter into the prepared pan.

(RECIPE CONTINUES)

Bake for 60 to 70 minutes, until the cake pulls away from the sides of the pan, springs back when you touch it, and a wooden skewer inserted in the center comes out clean. Transfer the pan to the prepared rack and let cool for 15 minutes. Invert the cake onto the rack and let cool completely.

MEANWHILE, MAKE THE GLAZE: In a small saucepan, combine the berries with the water and cook over medium heat, using a spoon to press on the berries, until they're broken down and have released lots of juice, about 5 minutes. Strain into a small bowl, pressing on the solids to release as much of the color as possible (it's okay if a few seeds make it through).

Sift the confectioners' sugar into a medium bowl. Add 2 tablespoons of the berry juice and mix until a smooth glaze forms.

When the cake is cool, drizzle the glaze on top and let it drip down the sides.

POTLUCK PREP. The unglazed cake can be covered and kept at room temperature overnight. Glaze within a few hours of serving.

PEACH-BLUEBERRY SLAB PIE
WITH SWEET ALMOND CRUST

VEGETARIAN / MAKES ONE 10 × 15-INCH PIE

FOR THE CRUST

1 CUP ICE WATER

2 TABLESPOONS CIDER VINEGAR

4 CUPS ALL-PURPOSE FLOUR

1 CUP ALMOND MEAL

3 TABLESPOONS GRANULATED SUGAR

1 TABLESPOON KOSHER SALT

2 CUPS (1 POUND; 4 STICKS) UNSALTED BUTTER, CUT INTO SMALL PIECES AND COLD

FOR THE PIE

6 SMALL TO MEDIUM PEACHES, PITTED AND CHOPPED (ABOUT 6 CUPS)

2 CUPS BLUEBERRIES

¼ CUP GRANULATED SUGAR

¼ CUP CORNSTARCH

JUICE OF ½ LEMON (ABOUT 1 TABLESPOON)

¼ TEASPOON KOSHER SALT

ALL-PURPOSE FLOUR, FOR DUSTING

1 LARGE EGG LIGHTLY BEATEN WITH 1 TABLESPOON WATER

3 TABLESPOONS TURBINADO SUGAR (SUGAR IN THE RAW) OR GRANULATED SUGAR

The trickiest part of making a slab pie is rolling out the dough to such large rectangles. With a little encouragement from baking genius Alice Medrich's blog, I started rolling the dough between floured sheets of plastic wrap or parchment paper. This made it easier to maneuver and pop in the fridge, if necessary, to keep the butter from melting. A classic slab pie is also known as a crust-lover's pie because the filling is fairly thin—it's like a giant Pop-Tart. If you'd like a thicker, juicier filling, add 2 more cups of blueberries and another tablespoon of cornstarch. And make sure to set a sheet of foil or a baking sheet on the bottom of your oven to catch any spillage!

PREPARE THE DOUGH: In a liquid measuring cup, combine the ice water with the vinegar.

In a large bowl, whisk the flour with the almond meal, sugar, and salt. Add the butter and use a pastry blender or your fingers to work it into the flour until most of it is the size of peas, with a few larger chunks remaining. Mix in the vinegar mixture, by tablespoon, until the dough just starts to hold together with a few dry spots remaining (this will happen somewhere between 12 and 16 tablespoons; see Note). Transfer half the dough to a large sheet of plastic wrap and gently knead to bring in any ragged edges. Pat the dough into a rectangle, wrap in plastic, and refrigerate for at least 1 hour or for up to 3 days. Repeat with the remaining dough.

ASSEMBLE AND BAKE THE PIE: Remove one piece of dough from the refrigerator and roll it out between 2 floured sheets of plastic wrap or parchment paper until you have an 18 × 13-inch rectangle. If the dough starts feeling too soft as you're rolling, refrigerate it for 15 to 20 minutes

(RECIPE CONTINUES)

until it firms up again. Fit the dough into a 15 × 10-inch baking sheet (also known as a jelly-roll pan), leaving any excess intact, and refrigerate.

In a bowl, toss the peaches with the blueberries, sugar, cornstarch, lemon juice, and salt.

Roll out the second piece of dough to a 16 × 11-inch rectangle. Spread the filling out in the crust-lined pan. Drape the second piece of dough on top of the filling. Roll and pinch the excess crust inward to create an edge around the pan. Use a sharp knife to cut vents all over the top crust. Refrigerate the assembled pie for 20 minutes.

Meanwhile, arrange a rack in the bottom of the oven and another in the center. Preheat the oven to 425°F.

Brush the top pastry with the egg wash and sprinkle with the turbinado sugar.

Bake the pie on the bottom rack of the oven for about 25 minutes. Reduce the temperature to 375°F and move the pie to the center rack. Bake for 30 to 35 more minutes, until the pastry is golden brown and the juices are bubbling. Let the pie cool on a wire rack for at least 2 hours before serving.

NOTE. After making pie dough for several years in the food processor, I've come to prefer preparing it by hand. I feel like it gives me more control over when to stop adding the liquid. If you prefer the food processor method, by all means, go for it.

POTLUCK PREP. To make this pie for an afternoon party, prepare and possibly even roll out the pie crust the night before. This way, you'll have enough time for your pie to cool. The baked pie will keep at room temperature for at least 2 days and can be refrigerated for at least 3 days. Any leftovers can be cut into individual squares, wrapped in plastic, and frozen; thaw on the counter.

ON FRUIT SALAD

In the fruit salads of my youth, I'd often find hard, white-fleshed, out-of-season strawberries mingling with whole grapes, mealy apples, soggy bananas, and cubes of vapid melons. There was rarely any thought given to seasonality. Sometimes the fruit had been tossed with sugar, or maybe some orange juice, but little else.

What started off as my trying to create a single fruit salad recipe became more of a blueprint for creating your own version. Your first move is to start with amazing fruit. In the summer, that's easy for a lot of us. In the winter, don't be afraid to look to sunnier places for inspiration. Here, I've outlined how to best prep your fruit, given you some syrups to dress them up, and offered ways to combine them. And unless you're serving your salad right away, skip the bananas. The texture suffers fast when it mingles with other fruit.

FRUIT OPTIONS BY SEASON

WINTER/SPRING

CITRUS. Use a sharp knife to peel the fruit and all of the bitter white pith. Then you can either cut the fruit into rounds or cut between the membranes to release the sections.

PINEAPPLE. Use a serrated knife to remove the peel. Cut the pineapple off of the core, and then slice as desired.

KIWI. Use a paring knife or peeler to peel and slice the fruit into rounds or half moons.

SPRING/SUMMER

STRAWBERRIES. Hull the strawberries, and then quarter if large or halve if small.

MANGO. Slice the short ends off the mango to give yourself a stable base. Use a sharp knife to remove the skin. Cut down along the pit to remove the flesh in as large of chunks as possible. Thinly slice or chop.

RASPBERRIES, BLACKBERRIES, BLUEBERRIES, AND THE LIKE. Leave them whole.

PEACHES, NECTARINES, AND PLUMS. Peel, if desired (it's not necessary!), and then halve, remove the pit, and cut into wedges.

CHERRIES. Stick with the sweet cherries for fruit salad. Halve and pit them.

MELONS. Halve, remove the seeds, and then cut into wedges. Cut the melon off of the rind and then into 1-inch pieces. A 3-pound cantaloupe usually yields 5 to 6 cups fruit.

FALL

GRAPES. Halve them, or slice into rounds.

APPLES. Skip Red Delicious apples in favor of something crunchier, like Gala or Honey Crisp. Peel if desired, then slice or cut into ½-inch pieces. Dress with lemon juice to prevent them from browning.

PEARS. Peel if desired, and cut into wedges or ½-inch pieces. Bosc pears usually hold up best in fruit salads.

SYRUPS FOR DRESSING FRUIT SALADS

GINGER-LIME SYRUP
MAKES ABOUT ½ CUP

Slice 1 inch of fresh ginger into ¼-inch pieces. In a small saucepan, combine ½ cup sugar (brown sugar works well if you don't mind the brown color in your salad) with ¼ cup water and the ginger, and cook over medium heat, stirring, until the sugar is dissolved, 3 minutes. Turn off the heat, and then add ¼ cup fresh lime juice. Let cool. Strain, pressing on the solids. Refrigerate for up to 1 week.

RHUBARB SYRUP
MAKES ABOUT 1 CUP

In a saucepan, combine ½ pound chopped rhubarb with ¾ cup sugar, ¾ cup water, and a pinch of salt, and bring to a boil over high heat. Reduce the heat to medium-low and simmer, stirring occasionally, until the fruit is very soft, 20 minutes. Strain the syrup through a sieve into a heatproof bowl or container, pressing on the solids. Stir in 1 tablespoon lemon juice. Let cool. Refrigerate for up to 1 week. (Add any extra to sparkling water or wine!)

HONEY-VANILLA SYRUP
MAKES ABOUT ½ CUP

In a small saucepan, melt ¼ cup plus 2 tablespoons honey with the same amount of water over medium heat. Add 1 split vanilla bean, remove the pan from the heat, and let cool. Refrigerate for up to 2 weeks.

ROSEMARY SYRUP
MAKES ABOUT ½ CUP

In a small saucepan, combine ½ cup water with ½ cup sugar and bring to a boil over high heat, stirring to dissolve the sugar. Add 1 large rosemary sprig, remove the pan from the heat, and let stand for 10 minutes. Discard the rosemary sprig. Refrigerate for up to 1 week.

SPICED SYRUP
MAKES ABOUT ½ CUP

In a small saucepan, combine ½ cup sugar, ½ cup water, 1 cinnamon stick, and 1 star anise, and bring to a boil over high heat, stirring to dissolve the sugar. Remove the pan from the heat and let cool. Strain into a small pitcher or liquid measuring cup and discard the spices. Refrigerate for up to 2 weeks.

TIPS FOR A GREAT FRUIT SALAD

1. For every 2 cups of fruit, add 1 tablespoon syrup, if using.

2. Fruit salad usually tastes best when the fruit is given a chance to macerate in the syrup at room temperature for at least 1 hour before chilling. But don't let it hang around too long; the salad is usually best the day it's made.

3. In addition to seasonality, think about colors that look good together. I love the look of a fruit salad that uses the same color fruit in different shades.

4. Add any herbs or crunchy ingredients like toasted nuts and seeds just before serving.

5. A pinch of salt rarely hurts.

6. Booze, sometimes, is good as well. Add a splash of bourbon to peach salads or light rum to berries.

7. You can actually roast or grill sturdy fruit, like wedges or halves of peaches, plums, or pears. Brush lightly with oil or butter and roast at 400°F for about 15 minutes, until tender and just starting to brown, or grill over medium heat, turning once, for 6 to 8 minutes.

8. You can toss everything together in a bowl or arrange it prettily on a platter and drizzle with the syrup.

SOME OF MY FAVORITE FRUIT SALAD COMBINATIONS

1. Mixed citrus or roasted pears + Rosemary Syrup + pecans

2. Mixed melons, or peaches, or pineapple and mango + Ginger-Lime Syrup + torn mint or basil + black pepper

3. Berries (of any sort) + Rhubarb Syrup + chopped pistachios+ crumbled meringues

4. Cherries + plums + Spiced Syrup + torn mint leaves

5. Peaches + Honey-Vanilla Syrup + bourbon + torn basil leaves

6. Roasted apples and pears + Honey-Vanilla Syrup + hazelnuts

PLUM-GINGER COFFEE CAKE
WITH COCONUT

VEGETARIAN / MAKES ONE 9 × 13-INCH CAKE

FOR THE STREUSEL

1 CUP ALL-PURPOSE FLOUR

½ CUP PACKED DARK BROWN SUGAR

1 TEASPOON GROUND GINGER

½ TEASPOON KOSHER SALT

½ CUP (1 STICK) UNSALTED BUTTER, MELTED

1 CUP FLAKED COCONUT, PREFERABLY UNSWEETENED

¼ CUP FINELY CHOPPED CRYSTALLIZED GINGER

FOR THE CAKE

1 CUP (2 STICKS) UNSALTED BUTTER, SOFTENED, PLUS MORE FOR THE PAN

2½ CUPS ALL-PURPOSE FLOUR

1 TEASPOON BAKING POWDER

¾ TEASPOON BAKING SODA

1 TEASPOON KOSHER SALT

1½ CUPS GRANULATED SUGAR

3 LARGE EGGS

1¼ CUPS SOUR CREAM

2 TEASPOONS PURE VANILLA EXTRACT

2 LARGE PLUMS (¾ POUND), CHOPPED INTO BITE-SIZE PIECES

When I tried the sour cream coffee cake recipe by my friend Justin Chapple (who contributed the Chard Slab Pie, page 183), it was absolutely perfect—rich and moist but not overly dense. I admit it, I totally swiped it and created a new topping—one that's studded with sweet plums, toasted coconut, and punchy caramelized ginger. Instead of plums, you can use pears or peaches.

POTLUCK PREP. The coffee cake is best the day it's made, but can be stored, covered, at room temperature for up to 2 days. If you prefer to pull the cake out of the pan, line the pan with parchment paper, leaving overhang on the long sides.

PREPARE THE STREUSEL: Use a fork to mix the flour with the brown sugar, ginger, and salt. Drizzle in the melted butter and stir until it resembles a clumpy dough. Add the coconut and crystallized ginger, and use your fingers to break the mixture into clumps. Refrigerate.

Preheat the oven to 350°F. Butter a 9 × 13-inch metal baking pan.

MAKE THE CAKE: In a medium bowl, whisk the flour with the baking powder, baking soda, and salt. In a large bowl and using an electric mixer, beat the 1 cup butter with the sugar at medium speed until fluffy, 2 minutes. Beat in the eggs, one at a time, and then the sour cream and vanilla. Beat the dry ingredients into the batter in 3 additions until just incorporated. Scrape the batter into the pan and spread it to the edges.

Add the plums to the streusel mixture and toss. Sprinkle the topping evenly over the batter.

Bake the cake for about 1 hour and 15 minutes, until the crumb topping is browned and a cake tester inserted in the center of the cake comes out clean. Transfer to a wire rack and let cool completely. Cut into squares and serve.

APPLE AND PEAR CRISP
WITH DATES AND HALVAH

VEGETARIAN / MAKES ONE 9 × 13-INCH CRISP

FOR THE FILLING

UNSALTED BUTTER, FOR THE PAN

2 POUNDS MIXED APPLES (4 TO 5), SUCH AS MACOUN AND GOLDEN DELICIOUS, PEELED, CORED, AND CHOPPED INTO LARGE CHUNKS

2 POUNDS PEARS (4 LARGE), SUCH AS BARTLETT OR ANJOU, PEELED, CORED, AND CHOPPED INTO LARGE CHUNKS

8 SOFT MEDJOOL DATES, PITTED AND FINELY CHOPPED (OPTIONAL)

¼ CUP HONEY

¼ CUP SUGAR

2 TABLESPOONS FRESH LEMON JUICE

¼ TEASPOON KOSHER SALT

FOR THE TOPPING

1 CUP ALL-PURPOSE FLOUR

1 CUP OLD-FASHIONED ROLLED OATS

¾ CUP SUGAR

1 TEASPOON KOSHER SALT

1 TEASPOON GROUND CINNAMON

½ TEASPOON GROUND GINGER

¾ CUP (1½ STICKS) UNSALTED BUTTER, CUT INTO ½-INCH PIECES

1 (3½-OUNCE) STICK HALVAH (ABOUT ½ CUP), BROKEN INTO CHUNKS

PLAIN YOGURT, CRÈME FRAÎCHE, OR ICE CREAM, FOR SERVING

Crisps are definitely the lazy person's fruit dessert. With no fussy crust to mess with, they come together quickly. For this topping, I added crumbled halvah, a Middle Eastern sesame candy that's sold on the counter of my corner deli and in the kosher section of many supermarkets. If you can't find it, leave it out and increase the sugar and butter in the topping by ¼ cup each.

POTLUCK PREP. The crisp tastes best the day it's made, but can be refrigerated for up to 3 days. Rewarm, if desired.

Preheat the oven to 350°F. Butter a 9 × 13-inch baking pan.

MAKE THE FILLING: In a large bowl, toss the apples, pears, and dates with the honey, sugar, lemon juice, and salt. Spread the mixture in the prepared pan.

MAKE THE TOPPING: In a bowl, whisk the flour with the oats, sugar, salt, cinnamon, and ginger. Add the butter and halvah and use your fingers to work it into the flour until it resembles coarse meal. Press the topping into clumps, and then scatter it over the filling.

Bake for about 50 minutes, until the filling is bubbling and the top is golden brown. Let cool for at least 20 minutes, and then serve warm or at room temperature with yogurt, crème fraîche, or ice cream.

CRANBERRY JAM STREUSEL BARS
WITH WALNUTS

VEGETARIAN / MAKES ONE 9 × 13-INCH PAN OF BARS

- 1 CUP (2 STICKS) UNSALTED BUTTER, MELTED, PLUS MORE FOR THE PAN
- 2¼ CUPS ALL-PURPOSE FLOUR
- 1¾ CUPS OLD-FASHIONED ROLLED OATS

- ½ CUP GRANULATED SUGAR
- ½ CUP LIGHT BROWN SUGAR
- 1½ TEASPOONS KOSHER SALT
- ¾ TEASPOON BAKING SODA

- 2 CUPS VANILLA-SPICED CRANBERRY JAM (PAGE 229) OR OTHER JAM
- ½ CUP WALNUTS, ROUGHLY CHOPPED

When it's sandwiched between layers of buttery streusel, sweet-tart cranberry jam becomes delicious and definitely dessert worthy. The jam comes together in just a few minutes, and you can pop it in the refrigerator or freezer to cool slightly while you make the crust. If you'd rather use another jam, including store-bought, by all means, do so. The bars will likely be sweeter, depending on how sugary the jam is.

POTLUCK PREP. The bars are best the day they're made, but can be covered and held at room temperature for up to 2 days.

Preheat the oven to 350°F. Butter a 9 × 13-inch baking pan and line it with parchment paper so an inch or so hangs over each of the long sides.

In a large bowl, mix the flour with the oats, sugars, salt, and baking soda. Pour the 1 cup melted butter over the mixture and stir until the flour is evenly moistened. Press all but about ¾ cup of the streusel in an even layer into the prepared pan. Spread the jam on top of the layer. Press the remaining streusel into clumps, add the walnuts, and toss. Sprinkle the walnut streusel all over the jam.

Bake the bars for about 45 minutes, until the top is golden brown. Transfer to a wire rack and let cool completely before cutting into squares.

TRIPLE COCONUT RICE PUDDING
WITH MANGO AND LIME

VEGAN; GLUTEN-FREE / SERVES 6 TO 12

FOR THE RICE PUDDING

1 CUP SUSHI RICE OR ARBORIO RICE

4 CUPS COCONUT WATER

1 (14-OUNCE) CAN COCONUT MILK

¼ CUP SUGAR

1 TEASPOON KOSHER SALT

FOR THE MANGO TOPPING

4 LARGE MANGOS, CUT INTO BITE-SIZE PIECES

ZEST FROM 1 LIME

1 TABLESPOON FRESH LIME JUICE

1 TABLESPOON SUGAR

TOASTED UNSWEETENED COCONUT FLAKES, FOR SERVING (OPTIONAL)

This vegan *and* gluten-free dessert is inspired by one of my favorite treats: Thai sticky rice and mango. To keep the pudding creamy even when it's chilled, some of the liquid gets mixed in after the pudding is cool. If your crowd is more health conscious, substitute quinoa for the rice. For a deeper flavor, use brown sugar.

POTLUCK PREP. The pudding and topping can be refrigerated overnight. Let the pudding stand at room temperature for at least 20 minutes before serving.

MAKE THE RICE PUDDING: In a strainer, rinse the rice well and set aside.

In a medium saucepan, combine the coconut water, coconut milk, sugar, and salt and cook over moderate heat, stirring, until the coconut milk melts. Ladle out about 1 cup of liquid into a measuring cup.

Add the rice to the saucepan and bring to a boil over high heat; simmer over medium heat, stirring occasionally, until the rice is tender and the pudding is thickened, about 20 minutes. Let the pudding cool until it's just above room temperature (about 30 minutes), and then stir in the remaining liquid until incorporated.

MEANWHILE, PREPARE THE MANGO TOPPING: In a bowl, toss the mango with the lime zest, lime juice, and sugar; let stand at room temperature for at least 20 minutes.

Serve the pudding at room temperature or refrigerate until lightly chilled (about 2 hours). Serve with the mango topping and, if using, the toasted coconut flakes.

RYE-MAPLE BANANA BREAD

VEGETARIAN / MAKES ONE 8½ × 4½-INCH LOAF

- 6 TABLESPOONS (¾ STICK) UNSALTED BUTTER, MELTED, PLUS MORE FOR THE PAN
- ¾ CUP ALL-PURPOSE FLOUR, PLUS MORE FOR DUSTING

- ¾ CUP WHOLE-GRAIN RYE FLOUR
- 1 TEASPOON BAKING SODA
- ¼ TEASPOON KOSHER SALT

- 2 LARGE, VERY RIPE BANANAS, MASHED (ABOUT 1 HEAPING CUP)
- ¾ CUP PURE MAPLE SYRUP
- 2 LARGE EGGS, LIGHTLY BEATEN

This simple banana bread is my ode to the Northeast, where maple syrup and rye berries both thrive. The flavors also happen to work beautifully together, creating a banana bread that's at once indulgent and wholesome.

POTLUCK PREP. The banana bread is actually tastier the day after it's made. Tightly wrapped, it will stay fresh for at least 3 days.

Preheat the oven to 325°F. Butter and flour an 8½ ×4½-inch metal loaf pan.

In a medium bowl, whisk the ¾ cup all-purpose flour with the rye flour, baking soda, and salt.

In a separate bowl, whisk the 6 tablespoons butter with the mashed bananas, maple syrup, and eggs. Stir the banana mixture into the dry ingredients. Scrape the batter into the prepared pan and smooth the top.

Bake, rotating the pan halfway through, for 45 to 55 minutes, until the bread is golden and a wooden skewer inserted into the center of the loaf comes out clean. Transfer to a wire rack and let cool for 15 minutes. Turn the bread out onto a plate and invert onto the rack to cool. Slice and serve warm or at room temperature.

VEGAN VARIATION. To cut the butter, substitute the same amount of safflower or coconut oil. To make the cake egg-free, you can substitute a chia seed gel: soak 2 tablespoons of ground chia seeds in 6 tablespoons of water for at least 10 minutes, then mix it into the batter.

LEMON–OLIVE OIL ZUCCHINI BREAD

VEGETARIAN / MAKES ONE 8½ × 4½-INCH LOAF

- ½ CUP EXTRA-VIRGIN OLIVE OIL, PLUS MORE FOR THE PAN
- ½ POUND ZUCCHINI (1 MEDIUM)
- 1 CUP ALL-PURPOSE FLOUR
- 1 CUP WHOLE WHEAT FLOUR

- ¼ CUP FINELY GRATED PARMIGIANO-REGGIANO CHEESE (ABOUT ½ OUNCE)
- 1½ TEASPOONS BAKING POWDER
- ½ TEASPOON BAKING SODA
- ½ TEASPOON KOSHER SALT

- ½ CUP HONEY
- ¼ CUP SUGAR
- ½ CUP SOUR CREAM OR FULL-FAT YOGURT
- 2 LARGE EGGS
- FINELY GRATED ZEST OF 1 LEMON

Zucchini bread sounds virtuous—it's made with vegetables—but it's usually just cake that's often a little ho-hum. I wanted to create a zucchini bread that is more delicious than the usual and, perhaps, a bit healthier thanks to the addition of whole wheat flour. This zucchini bread is supremely moist because of the sour cream and olive oil, and the honey gives it a rich flavor. Don't be put off by the Parmesan cheese in the batter; it provides an intriguing complexity without making the bread taste cheesy.

POTLUCK PREP. The bread is delicious the day it's made, and even tastier the following day. Tightly wrapped, it will stay fresh for at least 3 days.

Preheat the oven to 325°F. Generously oil a 8½ × 4½-inch metal loaf pan.

Coarsely grate the zucchini on the large holes of a box grater.

In a large bowl, whisk the flours with the cheese, baking powder, baking soda, and salt.

In a medium bowl, whisk the honey with the sugar, the ½ cup olive oil, the sour cream, eggs, and lemon zest. Add the wet ingredients to the dry ingredients and gently fold to combine. Scrape the batter into the prepared pan and smooth the top.

Bake, rotating the pan halfway through, for 60 to 70 minutes, until a skewer inserted in the center comes out clean. Let cool in the pan for 10 minutes, and then invert it onto a plate and back onto the rack to cool completely. Serve the bread at room temperature.

APPLESAUCE CHOCOLATE CHIP BUNDT CAKE

VEGETARIAN / MAKES 1 BUNDT CAKE

UNSALTED BUTTER OR BAKING SPRAY, FOR THE PAN

1½ CUPS ALL-PURPOSE FLOUR, PLUS MORE FOR DUSTING

1 CUP WHOLE WHEAT FLOUR

1½ CUPS GRANULATED SUGAR

2 TEASPOONS BAKING SODA

2 TEASPOONS GROUND CINNAMON

1 TEASPOON GROUND CARDAMOM

1 TEASPOON KOSHER SALT

½ TEASPOON GROUND CLOVES

½ TEASPOON FRESHLY GROUND BLACK PEPPER

2 CUPS UNSWEETENED APPLESAUCE

1 CUP SAFFLOWER OIL OR COCONUT OIL, OR ½ CUP EACH MELTED BUTTER AND OIL

2 LARGE EGGS, LIGHTLY BEATEN

1 (12-OUNCE) BAG SEMISWEET CHOCOLATE CHIPS

CONFECTIONERS' SUGAR, FOR DUSTING

A version of this one-bowl cake has been my absolute favorite since I was a kid. It's moist and spicy, with just the right amount of chocolate so it's not overwhelming, and it holds up for days on the counter (if you can resist eating all of it at once). I've since updated the recipe a little, dialing back the sugar a bit, adding black pepper and cardamom to the spice blend, and using some whole wheat flour.

POTLUCK PREP. The cake can be stored covered at room temperature for up to 3 days.

Preheat the oven to 350°F. Generously butter and flour a 12-cup Bundt pan or use baking spray with flour. (I mean it! This is the cake's one challenge—it tends to stick, so the more you grease, the better.)

In a large bowl, whisk the flours with the sugar, baking soda, cinnamon, cardamom, salt, cloves, and pepper. Whisk in the applesauce, oil, and eggs. Fold in the chocolate chips. Scrape the batter into the prepared pan.

Bake for 1 hour and 15 minutes, or until a wooden skewer inserted in the center comes out with a few crumbs attached. Transfer to a wire rack and let cool for 10 minutes. Invert the cake onto the rack and let cool completely. Sift confectioners' sugar over the cake, slice, and serve.

VEGAN VARIATION. If you want to make this cake egg-free, you can substitute a chia seed gel for the eggs: use 2 tablespoons of ground chia seeds soaked in 6 tablespoons water for at least 10 minutes.

BOURBON-PECAN CAKE
WITH CHOCOLATE CHUNKS

VEGETARIAN / MAKES ONE 9-INCH CAKE

½ CUP (1 STICK) UNSALTED BUTTER, CUT INTO SMALL PIECES AND SOFTENED, PLUS MORE FOR THE PAN

9 OUNCES PECANS (ABOUT 1¾ CUPS)

1 CUP PLUS 2 TABLESPOONS GRANULATED SUGAR

3 LARGE EGGS, AT ROOM TEMPERATURE

2 TABLESPOONS BOURBON

⅓ CUP ALL-PURPOSE FLOUR

¼ TEASPOON BAKING POWDER

3 OUNCES BITTERSWEET CHOCOLATE, FINELY CHOPPED (ABOUT ¾ CUP)

CONFECTIONERS' SUGAR, FOR DUSTING (OPTIONAL)

This decadent, slightly boozy cake is based on an Italian-style almond torte, in which the nuts are ground and act as most of the "flour." To get the nuts to the right consistency, you do need a food processor or powerful blender. Or, you can substitute pecan meal, which the King Arthur Flour company (kingarthurflour.com) makes, or any other nut meal. Then just mix up the cake in bowls.

POTLUCK PREP. The cake is best within 48 hours of baking, but can be wrapped and held at room temperature for up to 5 days.

Preheat the oven to 350°F. Butter a 9-inch round cake pan and line the bottom with parchment paper. Butter the paper.

Sprinkle ½ cup of the pecans in the pan and dust with 2 tablespoons of the granulated sugar.

In a food processor, pulse the remaining pecans with the remaining 1 cup sugar until the mixture resembles wet sand. Add the ½ cup butter, the eggs, and bourbon and pulse until smooth. Add the flour and baking powder and pulse just until incorporated. Add the chocolate and pulse just until incorporated (a few pulses). Scrape the batter into the prepared pan and smooth the top.

Bake in the lower third of the oven, rotating the pan halfway through, for about 50 minutes, until a wooden skewer inserted in the center of the cake comes out clean. Let cool in the pan for 10 minutes. Invert the cake onto a serving plate or board and peel off the parchment paper. Dust the cake with the confectioners' sugar, if desired, and serve warm or at room temperature.

SWEET AND SALTY PISTACHIO-CARDAMOM SHORTBREAD

VEGETARIAN / MAKES 24 COOKIES

1 CUP UNSALTED RAW
PISTACHIOS (ABOUT
4½ OUNCES)

1¼ CUPS ALL-PURPOSE FLOUR

½ CUP LIGHT BROWN SUGAR

¼ CUP CONFECTIONERS'
SUGAR

1 TEASPOON KOSHER SALT

½ TEASPOON GROUND
CARDAMOM

½ CUP (1 STICK) UNSALTED
BUTTER, COLD, CUT INTO
½-INCH PIECES

2 TO 3 TABLESPOONS
ICE WATER

I cannot resist shortbread or anything made with pistachios, so that's why you find them together here. These cookies are perfect for tea parties and other afternoon potlucks. If you're not opposed to a light floral flavor in your desserts, substitute ½ teaspoon rosewater for some of the ice water. If you prefer circular cookies, you can roll the dough into a log, and then slice the log into rounds.

POTLUCK PREP. The shortbread can be made up to 3 days in advance and kept in an airtight container at room temperature.

In a food processor, combine the pistachios with 1 tablespoon of the flour and process until finely ground. Add the rest of the flour, the sugars, salt, and cardamom and pulse to incorporate. Add the butter and pulse until most of it is the size of peas with a few larger chunks remaining. Pulse and gradually drizzle in enough of the ice water to form crumbs that are evenly moistened and hold together when pinched.

Line 2 baking sheets with parchment paper.

Turn out the dough onto a sheet of parchment paper set on a work surface and gently knead it together. Press the dough into a rectangle. Cover with another sheet of parchment paper, and then roll it ¼ inch thick (you should have about an 11 × 8-inch rectangle). Discard the top piece of parchment and trim the rough edges. Cut the dough into 24 bars. Poke the bars all over with a fork, and transfer to the prepared baking sheets, leaving some space between them. Refrigerate until firm, about 1 hour.

Preheat the oven to 350°F.

Bake the bars until golden, about 20 minutes. Transfer to a wire rack and let cool completely.

MEGAN'S CHOCOLATE CHERRY MILLET COOKIES

VEGETARIAN / MAKES ABOUT 15 COOKIES

- 1 CUP SPELT OR WHOLE WHEAT FLOUR
- ¼ CUP BARLEY FLOUR OR ALL-PURPOSE FLOUR
- ¾ CUP OLD-FASHIONED ROLLED OATS
- ⅓ CUP RAW MILLET
- ⅓ CUP UNSWEETENED COCOA POWDER

- ½ TEASPOON BAKING SODA
- ½ TEASPOON BAKING POWDER
- ½ TEASPOON GROUND GINGER
- ½ TEASPOON GROUND CINNAMON
- ½ TEASPOON KOSHER SALT
- ½ CUP COCONUT OIL, MELTED AND COOLED SLIGHTLY

- ½ CUP PURE MAPLE SYRUP
- 1 LARGE EGG, LIGHTLY BEATEN
- 1 TEASPOON PURE VANILLA EXTRACT
- ½ CUP DRIED CHERRIES
- ⅓ CUP DARK CHOCOLATE CHUNKS OR CHIPS

I feel a special connection with Megan Gordon, who created the blog *A Sweet Spoonful,* because we both write about food and own product-based businesses. Megan, a grain lover like me, is the master of the whole-grain cookie, and I was thrilled when she shared with me this soft double chocolate cookie recipe, which calls for, of all things, millet. It's adapted from a breakfast cookie in her first book, *Whole Grain Mornings.* She says, "These whole-grain cookies are especially great for outdoor or midday potlucks because they're not at all too sweet, and can double as a snack or a dessert."

POTLUCK PREP. The cookies will stay fresh in an airtight container for 3 to 4 days. You can also wrap the cookies in plastic wrap and freeze for up to 1 month.

Preheat the oven to 350°F. Line 2 large baking sheets with parchment paper.

In a large bowl, whisk together the flours, oats, millet, cocoa powder, baking soda, baking powder, ginger, cinnamon, and salt.

In a separate bowl, whisk the coconut oil with the maple syrup, egg, and vanilla. Add the wet mixture to the dry ingredients and fold together until incorporated. Stir in the cherries and chocolate chunks. Let the dough rest for 10 minutes.

For each cookie, scoop out 2 to 3 tablespoons of dough and, working quickly, form a ball with the palms of your hands. Place the balls about 1½ inches apart on the prepared baking sheet and gently flatten with the palm of your hand until about ¾ inch thick.

Bake for 11 to 14 minutes, until the tops of the cookies are dry and the edges feel slightly firm to the touch, yet still slightly soft in the center (they'll continue firming up as they cool). Let cool for 10 minutes on the baking sheet, and then transfer to a wire rack to cool completely.

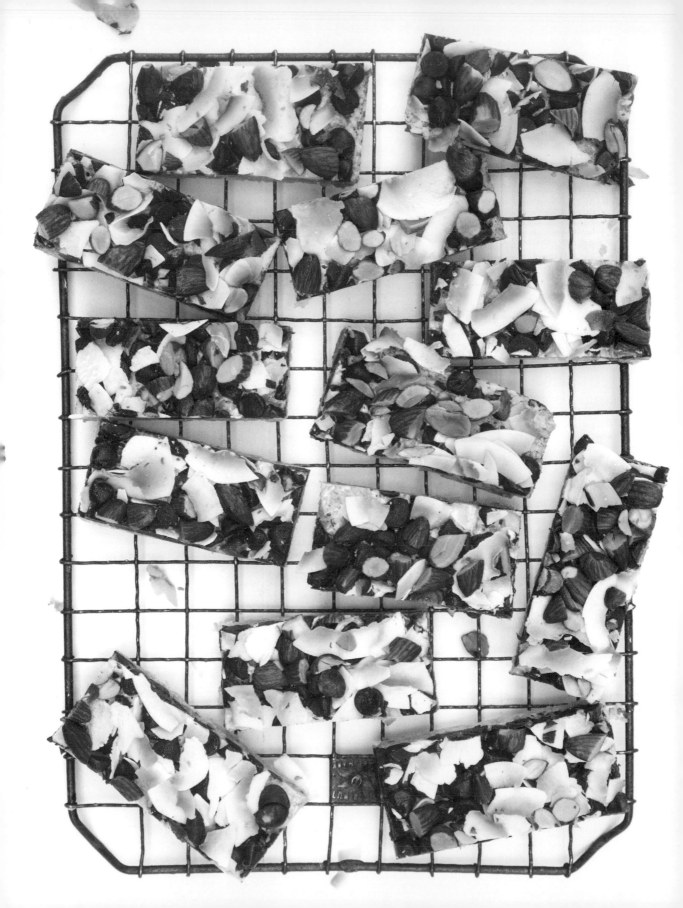

POTATO CHIP–CRUSTED MAGIC BARS

VEGETARIAN; GLUTEN-FREE (OPTIONAL) / MAKES ONE 9 × 13-INCH PAN OF BARS

- 1 (10-OUNCE) BAG PLAIN SALTED POTATO CHIPS, PREFERABLY NOT THICK-CUT
- 3 TABLESPOONS ALL-PURPOSE FLOUR OR RICE FLOUR

- 4 TABLESPOONS (½ STICK) UNSALTED BUTTER, MELTED
- 1 (14-OUNCE) CAN SWEETENED CONDENSED MILK
- 1 (12-OUNCE) BAG SEMI-SWEET CHOCOLATE CHIPS

- 1 CUP LARGE UNSWEETENED COCONUT FLAKES, SUCH AS BOB'S RED MILL, OR SWEETENED COCONUT FLAKES
- 1 CUP SALTED SMOKED ALMONDS, OR YOUR NUT OF CHOICE, ROUGHLY CHOPPED

Whether you call them magic bars or seven-layer (or sometimes five-layer) cookies, you probably know these treats. Chunky bits—like chocolate chips, nuts, and coconut—get layered over sticky condensed milk and a crisp cookie crust. The bars are perfect for potlucks because they're portable and super-easy to make. The problem is (for me!) that they're always way too sweet.

In this version, you'll find a potato chip crust, unsweetened coconut flakes, and salted smoked almonds. The bars are just as chewy, crunchy, and appealing as the usual but taste less sugary.

POTLUCK PREP. The bars can be served right from the pan, if desired. They can be wrapped in foil and held at room temperature for up to 3 days. They can also be cut into bars, individually wrapped in plastic, and frozen. They make for a chewy sweet treat right from the freezer.

Preheat the oven to 350°F. Butter a 9 × 13-inch baking pan, preferably metal, and line with parchment paper so it overhangs by a couple of inches on the long sides of the pan.

In a food processor, pulse the potato chips with the flour until they resemble coarse bread crumbs. Pour in the 4 tablespoons butter and pulse until the chips are evenly moistened and finely chopped. Press the mixture into the prepared baking pan.

Bake for about 15 minutes, until the crust is dry and very lightly browned. Let cool.

Pour the sweetened condensed milk over the crust and tip the pan so it forms an even layer. Scatter the chocolate chips, coconut, and nuts on top and use a fork or the back of a spoon to press the ingredients into the sticky condensed milk.

Bake for about 25 minutes, until the coconut is toasted and the condensed milk is lightly browned at the edges. Transfer to a rack and let cool.

When the bar is cool, use the parchment paper to lift it out of the pan. Cut into any size squares you desire and serve.

CONDIMENTS
AND OTHER THINGS IN JARS

SALT-AND-PEPPER CANDIED CASHEWS

VEGAN; GLUTEN-FREE / MAKES ABOUT 1½ CUPS

½ CUP SUGAR

½ CUP WATER

1 TEASPOON KOSHER SALT

¼ TEASPOON FRESHLY
GROUND BLACK PEPPER

1½ CUPS ROASTED UNSALTED
CASHEWS

These sweet and spicy nuts are a great easy hostess gift, but you can also serve them with cocktails or use them to garnish salads, like the Chinese Chicken Salad on page 77.

Line a large baking sheet with parchment paper.

In a small saucepan, combine the sugar and water and boil over medium-high heat until a deep amber caramel forms, about 6 minutes. Stir in the salt and pepper, followed by the cashews. Quickly spread the cashews onto the prepared baking sheet in a single layer. Let stand until cool, and then break up into pieces and serve.

POTLUCK PREP. The nuts can be kept in an airtight container for up to 2 days. Spread them on a baking sheet and dry them briefly in a 300°F oven if they become sticky.

SEASONING SALTS

Want to make the easiest potluck dish ever? Slice some tomatoes or halve hard-boiled eggs, sprinkle them with one of these salts, and you're done. Or use them as spice rubs for simple meat preparations. (See photograph on pages 218–219.)

SMOKY ORANGE SALT

VEGAN; GLUTEN-FREE /
MAKES A SCANT ¼ CUP

This alluring, punchy salt is delicious sprinkled over hard-boiled eggs, shrimp, tomatoes, roasted chicken, and roasted squash.

3 TABLESPOONS KOSHER SALT

1 TEASPOON FINELY GRATED ORANGE ZEST

1 TEASPOON FINELY CHOPPED FRESH ROSEMARY

½ TEASPOON SWEET SMOKED PAPRIKA

In a bowl, combine the salt, orange zest, rosemary, and paprika, tossing to make sure the zest doesn't clump. Toss occasionally for about 1 hour, until the zest feels dry. (Store in an airtight container for about 1 week.)

ZA'ATAR

VEGAN; GLUTEN-FREE /
MAKES ABOUT ¼ CUP

Once you start using this Middle Eastern blend, you just might find it hard to stop. I love sprinkling it over Greek yogurt and lots of different salads, like the simple Marinated Tomatoes with Za'atar (page 145). Sumac is a tart powder made from a dried berry, and unfortunately, there really isn't a substitute. You can omit it, but the flavor just won't be quite right. Luckily, the growing popularity of Middle Eastern food should make sumac— or even pre-blended za'atar—more widely available.

4 TEASPOONS SESAME SEEDS

1 TABLESPOON SUMAC

4 TEASPOONS DRIED THYME

2 TEASPOONS COARSE SEA SALT

1 TEASPOON DRIED OREGANO

In a small dry skillet, toast the sesame seeds over moderate heat until fragrant and lightly browned, 1 to 2 minutes. Immediately transfer to a mortar or a bowl and let cool.

Add the sumac, thyme, salt, and oregano to the sesame seeds and use a pestle or the bottom of an ice cream scoop to lightly pound everything together until some of the sesame seeds are broken. (Store in an airtight container for up to 1 month.)

SPICY FENNEL SALT

VEGAN; GLUTEN-FREE /
MAKES ABOUT ¼ CUP

This anise-y salt is inspired by the seasoning used for porchetta, the famous Italian pork roast. It's terrific on any meat, especially lamb and chicken.

2 TABLESPOONS KOSHER SALT

2 TABLESPOONS FENNEL SEEDS

¼ TEASPOON RED PEPPER FLAKES

Using a pestle or the bottom of an ice cream scoop, crush the salt, fennel seeds, and red pepper flakes together in a mortar or a bowl. (Store in an airtight container for up to 3 months.)

MY GREEN SAUCES

People who hate cilantro, I'm sorry. My love
for this fragrant herb borders on obsession. I
also happen to love cuisines that use tons of
cilantro—from Mexican to Middle Eastern to
Southeast Asian—so that fuels my (over?) use.
These green sauces are some of my favorite
garnishes for adding pop to simple roasted
meats, vegetables, or other recipes in this book.

thai-style chile relish

fresh tomatillo salsa

*cilantro-pumpkin
seed pesto*

FRESH TOMATILLO SALSA

VEGAN; GLUTEN-FREE /
MAKES ABOUT 1½ CUPS

This vibrant green salsa adds zing to the enchiladas on page 69, and is also just plain delicious for dipping chips. The more jalapeño seeds you add, the spicier it will be. If you want an even more fiery salsa, use a serrano chile instead.

- ¾ POUND TOMATILLOS, HUSKED AND ROUGHLY CHOPPED
- ¼ CUP ROUGHLY CHOPPED WHITE ONION
- ⅓ CUP FRESH CILANTRO LEAVES
- 1 JALAPEÑO, STEMMED, SEEDED IF DESIRED

In a food processor or blender, puree the tomatillos, onion, cilantro, and jalapeño. Add water, 1 tablespoon at a time, if needed to loosen the salsa; you should not need to add more than 4 tablespoons. (The salsa can be refrigerated in an airtight container for up to 3 days.)

CILANTRO–PUMPKIN SEED PESTO

VEGAN; GLUTEN-FREE /
MAKES ABOUT 1 CUP

I first noticed cilantro pesto with pumpkin seeds in Heidi Swanson's terrific *Supernatural Everyday* cookbook, where she tosses it with ravioli for a room-temperature salad. I created my own cheese-less version and put it on everything, from eggs to roasted chicken. In the dead of winter, this sauce makes roasted root vegetables taste bright and alive.

- 2 GARLIC CLOVES
- ½ CUP PUMPKIN SEEDS
- 3 CUPS LOOSELY PACKED FRESH CILANTRO LEAVES AND TENDER STEMS
- ¾ CUP OLIVE OIL
- 2 TEASPOONS FRESH LEMON JUICE, PLUS MORE TO TASTE

  KOSHER SALT AND FRESHLY GROUND BLACK PEPPER

Preheat the oven or toaster oven to 350°F.

In a small saucepan, bring some water to a boil. Add the garlic and boil for 1 minute. Drain and transfer to a blender; let cool (or run under cold water, then drain well).

Spread the pumpkin seeds on a baking sheet and toast in the oven until puffed, 2 to 3 minutes. Transfer to a blender and let cool. (Alternatively, you can toast the pumpkin seeds in a dry skillet.)

Add the cilantro and pulse until the garlic, pumpkin seeds, and cilantro are finely chopped. With the machine on, add the olive oil in a thin stream, and then add the lemon juice. Season with salt and pepper. (The pesto can be refrigerated in an airtight container for up to 3 days.)

PISTACHIO SALSA VERDE

GLUTEN-FREE / MAKES ABOUT ¾ CUP

As opposed to the Mexican salsa verde, which is more runny and made with tomatillos, the Mediterranean style is more like a pesto but with brighter flavors that come from capers, anchovies, and an acid. This version is made in a food processor, but if you have occasional masochistic tendencies in the kitchen, as I do, you can pound this in a mortar for a more rustic (and, I think, more interesting) texture.

Salsa verdes are incredibly versatile. This one goes with the brined pork loin on page 87, but it's equally good with any meat along with fish or cooked vegetables.

- 2 CUPS FRESH FLAT-LEAF PARSLEY LEAVES AND TENDER STEMS
- 2 OUNCES ROASTED PISTACHIOS, SHELLED (ABOUT ¼ CUP)
- 1 SMALL TO MEDIUM GARLIC CLOVE
- 1 TABLESPOON DRAINED CAPERS
- ½ ANCHOVY FILLET
- ½ CUP EXTRA-VIRGIN OLIVE OIL
- 1 TEASPOON FRESH LEMON JUICE
- KOSHER SALT
- RED PEPPER FLAKES (OPTIONAL)

In a mini food processor, pulse the parsley with the pistachios, garlic clove, capers, and anchovy until finely chopped. Add the olive oil and lemon juice and pulse just until blended. Transfer to a bowl and season with salt and red pepper flakes, if desired. (The salsa verde can be refrigerated in an airtight container overnight.)

GREEN CHUTNEY

VEGAN; GLUTEN-FREE /
MAKES ABOUT 1 CUP

This bright, lightly spicy sauce is terrific with the Samosa-Filling Stuffed Poblanos (page 113), or you can drizzle it over some roasted or grilled vegetables with dollops of yogurt. Add more chile seeds for a spicier sauce. If you prefer, you can swap some or all of the cilantro for mint leaves.

- ¼ CUP WATER
- 2 LOOSELY PACKED CUPS FRESH CILANTRO LEAVES
- 1 LARGE JALAPEÑO, HALVED, SOME OF THE SEEDS REMOVED, COARSELY CHOPPED
- 1 (2-INCH) PIECE FRESH GINGER, PEELED AND COARSELY CHOPPED
- ¼ CUP FRESH LEMON JUICE
- 2 TEASPOONS SUGAR
- KOSHER SALT

In a mini food processor, combine the water with the cilantro, jalapeño, ginger, lemon juice, and sugar and puree until nearly smooth. Season with salt and serve. (The chutney can be refrigerated in an airtight container overnight.)

THAI-STYLE CHILE RELISH

GLUTEN-FREE / MAKES ABOUT 1 CUP

This deeply flavored, bright, and funky condiment is inspired by *nam prik num,* a genre of chile relishes that are often served with sausage in Chiang Mai, Thailand. My version uses poblano chiles, which add more flavor than heat. If you'd like a more fiery version, grill and add a serrano chile to the mix. I like this sauce with beef or a platter of grilled vegetables.

3 LARGE GARLIC CLOVES, UNPEELED

3 POBLANO CHILES

1 CUP FRESH CILANTRO

2 TABLESPOONS ASIAN FISH SAUCE

1 TABLESPOON SUGAR

1 TABLESPOON FRESH LIME JUICE,
PLUS MORE FOR SEASONING

1 TABLESPOON VEGETABLE OIL

Preheat a grill or a grill pan.

Skewer the garlic. Grill the garlic and chiles over medium-high heat, turning frequently, until the garlic is charred and softened, about 5 minutes, and the chiles are blackened all over, about 10 minutes.

Transfer the vegetables to a plate. Peel the garlic and transfer to a food processor. Rub the skins off the chiles, and then core them, discarding most of the seeds. Add the flesh to the food processor. Pulse the garlic and chiles until coarsely chopped. Add the cilantro, fish sauce, sugar, and 1 tablespoon of lime juice and pulse to a chunky puree. Add the vegetable oil and process until incorporated. Season the relish with more lime juice, if desired, and serve. (The relish can be refrigerated in an airtight container overnight.)

green chutney

*pistachio
salsa verde*

VANILLA-SPICED CRANBERRY JAM

VEGAN; GLUTEN-FREE / MAKES ABOUT 2 CUPS

1 (12-OUNCE) BAG FRESH
CRANBERRIES

¾ CUP APPLE CIDER

¾ CUP SUGAR

1 VANILLA BEAN, SPLIT AND
SEEDS SCRAPED

⅛ TEASPOON CHINESE
FIVE-SPICE POWDER OR
GROUND CINNAMON

Cranberries don't need much simmering time or fuss to become jam, making this an easy but impressive thing to bring to a potluck. You can use the jam in the bar cookies on page 205, serve it with the Pumpkin Biscuits (page 175), or set it out with a cheese plate. If you want a more turkey-friendly jam (similar to cranberry sauce), leave out the vanilla and spices.

In a large saucepan, combine the cranberries, cider, sugar, vanilla bean and seeds, and five-spice powder, and bring to a boil over high heat, stirring to help the sugar dissolve. Simmer over medium heat until the cranberries start to burst and the jam is quite thick, 8 to 10 minutes. Use a slotted spoon to mash the cranberries as much as possible.

Let the jam cool slightly, then remove the vanilla bean pod. Transfer the jam to a pint jar or other container. (The jam can be covered and refrigerated for up to 2 weeks.)

QUICKEST STRAWBERRY JAM

VEGAN; GLUTEN-FREE / MAKES ABOUT 1½ CUPS

2 POUNDS STRAWBERRIES,
HULLED

½ CUP SUGAR

This is barely a recipe, but if it is actually a recipe, I have to credit Jamie Oliver for it. He made this on one of my favorite cooking shows, *Jamie at Home*. This is not a jam meant for long storage; it should be eaten within a week or so. It's terrific baked on top of the Strawberry Jam Cheesecake Bars (page 190) or swirled into Triple Coconut Rice Pudding (page 206). Packaged in a cute little jar, it also makes a great host gift. Just be sure it's kept in the refrigerator.

In a wide, nonreactive pan, combine the strawberries and sugar. Use your hands to mash the strawberries. Keep working until the mixture looks like a rough, liquidy jam and the sugar is dissolved. Bring the mixture to a simmer over medium heat and cook, skimming off the foam occasionally, until thickened and jammy, about 20 minutes. (The jam can be covered and refrigerated for about 1 week.)

VARIATION. To flavor the jam, try adding one of the following: ¼ teaspoon pink peppercorns; 1 thyme sprig (which you remove before eating); ½ teaspoon dried lavender; or a tiny pinch of ground cardamom.

ACKNOWLEDGMENTS

They say it takes a village to raise a child. This is even truer for a cookbook.

First, to my agent, Jonah Straus: We did it! After years of dance parties, cocktails, and brainstorming sessions, we finally had a chance to work together. Thank you for your encouragement and moral support throughout this entire process, from proposal to publication. I'm lucky to have you as an agent but even more lucky to count you as a friend.

To Rica Allannic, thank you for your support of *Modern Potluck* from the very start. It was an absolute dream that you acquired this book. Thank you to Doris Cooper, Anna Mintz, and Carly Gorga at Clarkson Potter for your enthusiasm. And Ashley Meyer—how lucky are we that Rica decided to take a sabbatical just as my book was being edited? It's been a delight working with you.

To my *Food & Wine* family: I never would have gotten here without you. Thank you especially to Dana Cowin, Pam Kaufman, and Kate Heddings for teaching me about high standards and for all of your support over the years. And to Tina Ujlaki: You are the world's best mentor and my second mother. I *know* that the recipes in this book are better because of your training.

Thank you as well to Marcia Kiesel, Grace Parisi, Melissa Rubel Jacobson, Justin Chapple, and Kay Chun—five incredible cooks and recipe developers. I learned so much about flavor and proper technique from you; tasting the food you worked each day was like getting a culinary graduate degree.

To Cherry Jones, our wonderful former nanny: Thank you for keeping my daughter happy, engaged, and healthy as I toiled away on this book. And for taking home so much of the extra food. (Thank you to Patrick Moroney and Jennifer Urbealis-Moroney for assisting with this difficult task as well!)

The photo shoot for this book required its own subsection of the village, but the days I spent working on it were some of my favorite during the process. Thank you to photographer Yossy Arefi for creating such gorgeous photos and for your expert styling. You work with such confidence and grace. Thank you to Paola Andrea for sourcing and sharing stunning props as well. Carrie Purcell: You made my food looked exactly as I imagined it but better than I ever could have styled it myself; it was a pleasure to watch you work.

Thank you to Mirella Cheeseman, Emma Saccone, Brooks Halliday, Monica Pierini, and Richard Lapham for your help with the photo shoots as well. To Michael Nagin, La Tricia Watford, Jan Derevjanik, Mark McCauslin, and Heather Williamson for creating and producing such a beautiful design. And to Lauren Velasquez and Sean Boyles, for handling marketing and publicity efforts, respectively.

To my friends and neighbors who appear in the photos: Charles Antin; Alessandra Bulow; Anna Watson Carl; Daniel Gritzer; Cherry Jones; Ellora Forrest; Sachin Hyjek; Rakhi Seth-Forrest; Patrick and Evie Moroney; Postell and Otis Pringle; Brainerd, Eloise, and Beatrix Taylor. Thank you for being part of this project!

Thank you to my volunteer recipe testers: Charles Antin, Jane Antin, Kate Brambilla, Jennifer Bee Barker, Maren Ellingboe, Gina Gancheva, Arielle Heller, Sara Hodgdon, Irene Lin, Jenn Louis, Joy Manning, Maggie Mariolis, Becky McCandless, Jennifer Urbealis-Moroney, Patrick Moroney, Amanda McFaul, Raquel Pelzel, Natalie Rockwell, Debra Kruth, Darcy Sawatzki, Rachael Shapiro, Natalia Stroutinsky, Emily Thelin, and Tracey Webber. Your feedback throughout this process was invaluable.

To Amelia Rampe: You are a superstar! Thank you for coming to my house, week after week for several months, to test recipes. I know that these recipes are even more delicious because of your help and that your career will take you to great places. Thank you Tessa Thompson at Institute of Culinary Education (my alma mater!) for connecting me with Amelia.

I was thrilled when many of my friends and favorite home cooks agreed to contribute recipes. Thank you to Anna Watson Carl, Justin Chapple, Clotilde Dusoulier, Megan Gordon, Daniel Gritzer, Phoebe Lapine, Heidi Swanson, and Molly Yeh for sharing your best potluck dishes.

To my first family: My parents and my sister, Katie. Thank you always for your support.

And to my second family, my husband and daughter, to whom I dedicate this book: Thank you a million times over for your love and encouragement. This never would have happened without you!

INDEX

Note: Page references in *italics* indicate photographs.